SAVING ENDANGERED SPECIES

THE MOUNTAIN GORILLA

Help Save This Endangered Species!

Alison Imbriaco

MyReportLinks.com Books
an imprint of

 Enslow Publishers, Inc.

Box 398, 40 Industrial Road
Berkeley Heights, NJ 07922
USA

MyReportLinks.com Books, an imprint of Enslow Publishers, Inc. MyReportLinks®
is a registered trademark of Enslow Publishers, Inc.

Library of Congress Cataloging-in-Publication Data

Imbriaco, Alison.
  The mountain gorilla : help save this endangered species! / Alison Imbriaco.
     p. cm. — (Saving endangered species)
  Includes bibliographical references and index.
  ISBN 1-59845-035-2
  1. Gorilla—Juvenile literature. I. Title. II. Series.
  QL737.P96I43 2006
  599.884—dc22
                                    2005018191

Printed in the United States of America

10 9 8 7 6 5 4 3 2 1

To Our Readers:
Through the purchase of this book, you and your library gain access to the Report Links that specifically back up this book.

The Publisher will provide access to the Report Links that back up this book and will keep these Report Links up to date on **www.myreportlinks.com** for five years from the book's first publication date.

We have done our best to make sure all Internet addresses in this book were active and appropriate when we went to press. However, the author and the Publisher have no control over, and assume no liability for, the material available on those Internet sites or on other Web sites they may link to.

The usage of the MyReportLinks.com Books Web site is subject to the terms and conditions stated on the Usage Policy Statement on **www.myreportlinks.com**.

A password may be required to access the Report Links that back up this book. The password is found on the bottom of page 4 of this book.

Any comments or suggestions can be sent by e-mail to comments@myreportlinks.com or to the address on the back cover.

Photo Credits: Adrian Warren, Last Refuge, Ltd., p. 17; African Wildlife Foundation, p. 75; AP/Wide World Photos, p. 72; Columbus Zoo, p. 24; Dian Fossey Gorilla Fund International, pp. 9, 21; Enslow Publishers, Inc., p. 5; Escape.com, p. 87; Exploring the Environment, p. 13; Fauna and Flora International, pp. 86, 94; Forest.org, p. 54; Gerry Ellis/Getty Images, pp. 1, 3, 14, 29, 32, 34, 38–39, 41, 43, 44–45, 66, 69, 78, 89, 102, 111; Informatics, pp. 11, 19; International Fund for Animal Welfare, p. 104; International Gorilla Conservation Programme, pp. 96, 109; Morris Animal Foundation, pp. 62, 110; MyReportLinks.com Books, p. 4; NASA, pp. 56, 92; *National Geographic,* p. 81; PBS, p. 59; Photos.com, p. 61; Rodrique Ngowi, AP/Wide World Photos, p. 101; Science in Africa, p. 22; Smithsonian Institution, The National Zoo, p. 70; The Bushmeat Project, p. 76; The Dian Fossey Gorilla Fund, p. 83; TRAFFIC, p. 91; United Nations Environment Programme, pp. 58, 98; University of Michigan, p. 30; USFWS, pp. 25, 115; Wildlife Conservation Society, pp. 37, 47, 52; Woods Hole Research Center, p. 107; World Wildlife Fund, p. 49.

Cover Photo: Gerry Ellis/Getty Images.

CONTENTS

MyReportLinks.com Books
Great Books, Great Links, Great for Research!

The Internet sites featured in this book can save you hours of research time. These Internet sites—we call them **"Report Links"**—are constantly changing, but we keep them up to date on our Web site.

When you see this "Approved Web Site" logo, you will know that we are directing you to a great Internet site that will help you with your research.

Give it a try! Type **http://www.myreportlinks.com** into your browser, click on the series title and enter the password, then click on the book title, and scroll down to the Report Links listed for this book.

The Report Links will bring you to great source documents, photographs, and illustrations. MyReportLinks.com Books save you time, feature Report Links that are kept up to date, and make report writing easier than ever! A complete listing of the Report Links can be found on pages 116–117 at the back of the book.

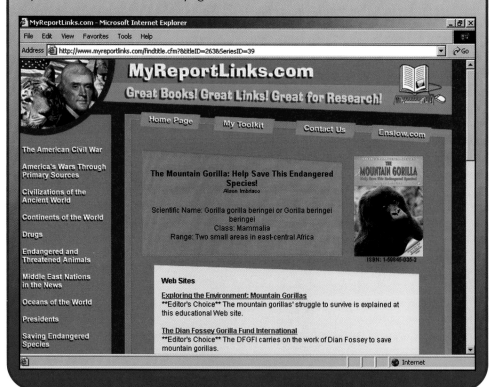

Please see "To Our Readers" on the copyright page for important information about this book, the MyReportLinks.com Web site, and the Report Links that back up this book.

Please enter SMG1685 if asked for a password.

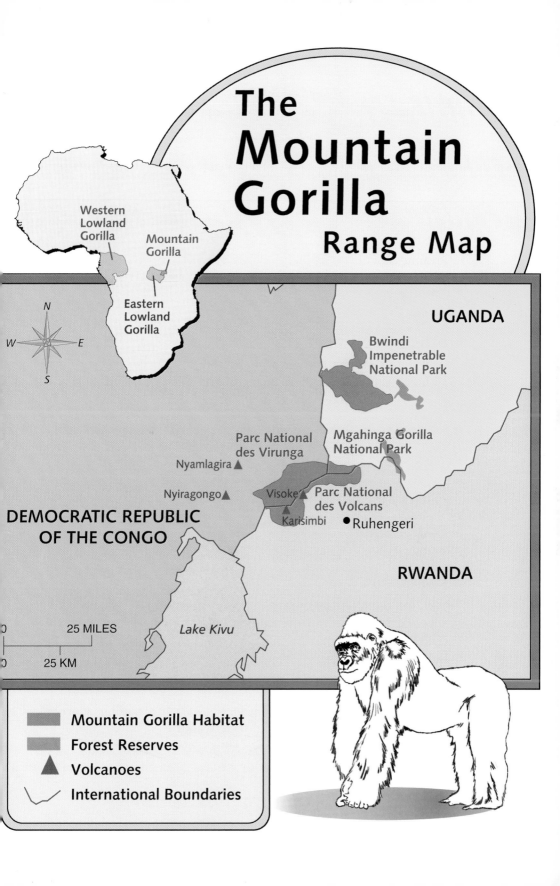

The Mountain Gorilla
Range Map

Western Lowland Gorilla

Mountain Gorilla

Eastern Lowland Gorilla

N
W — E
S

UGANDA

Bwindi Impenetrable National Park

Parc National des Virunga

Mgahinga Gorilla National Park

Nyamlagira ▲

Nyiragongo ▲

Visoke ▲

Parc National des Volcans

Karisimbi ▲

● Ruhengeri

DEMOCRATIC REPUBLIC OF THE CONGO

RWANDA

25 MILES

25 KM

Lake Kivu

Mountain Gorilla Habitat

Forest Reserves

▲ Volcanoes

International Boundaries

Mountain Gorilla Facts

▶ **Kingdom**
Animalia (animal)

▶ **Order**
Primates

▶ **Family**
Hominidae

▶ **Scientific Name**
Depending on the classification system, either *Gorilla gorilla beringei* or *Gorilla beringei beringei*. The Virunga population is classified as *Gorilla beringei beringei*.

▶ **Common Name**
Mountain gorilla

▶ **Swahili Name**
Gorila or N'gagi

▶ **Distribution**
Two small areas in east-central Africa

▶ **Population** (2005 census conducted by conservation groups)
700 individuals: 380 in the Virunga volcanoes region of Uganda, Rwanda, and the Democratic Republic of the Congo (DRC); 320 in the Bwindi Impenetrable National Park, Uganda.

▶ **Height**
Males—more than 5.5 feet (1.7 meters) when standing, more than 3 feet (.9 meter) when knuckle walking

▶ **Weight**
Males: 300 to 400 pounds (140 to 180 kilograms)
Females: 150 to 200 pounds (70 to 90 kilograms)

▶ Physical Description
Jet black hair, 3 to 4 inches (8 to 10 centimeters) long, covering much of their bodies; male and female do not look alike.

▶ Diet
Vegetarian

▶ Habitat
Mountain rain forests

▶ Predators
Leopards, humans

▶ Gestation
About nine months

▶ Size at Birth
About 4 to 5 pounds (1.8 to 2.3 kilograms)

▶ Status
Endangered throughout its range

▶ Life Span
About thirty-five years

▶ Threats
Loss of habitat, poaching, disease

No one who looks into a gorilla's eyes—intelligent, gentle, vulnerable—can remain unchanged, for the gap between ape and human vanishes.

George Schaller

SURPRISING SURVIVAL

Pablo was a mountain gorilla juvenile delinquent. That was the opinion of the researchers studying his family in its mountain rain-forest habitat during the late 1970s. Pablo liked to grab the knapsacks of passing researchers and, if he yanked hard enough, watch the researchers fall backward.[1] One afternoon he

Pablo's group of mountain gorillas appears in this photograph on the Web site of **The Dian Fossey Gorilla Fund International** (DFGFI). That organization carries on the work begun by Fossey in the 1960s.

EDITOR'S CHOICE

grabbed a researcher's notes, fled to safety beside his 350-pound father, and ate every page.[2]

Pablo tried the patience of gorilla mothers in his extended family when he played too enthusiastically with younger gorillas. A "cough grunt" is a sharp bark from deep within the chest that gorillas use to express annoyance. And cough grunts were often aimed at Pablo as mothers retrieved their offspring. A researcher wrote that she had the distinct impression that the entire gorilla family "would have been delighted if I had just stuck him into my knapsack" and kept him until he grew up.[3]

Amy Vedder, one of the gorilla researchers with the Karisoke Research Center in the central African country of Rwanda, finished her study of Pablo's family in 1979. As she left Karisoke, she wondered what would happen to the playful and energetic young gorilla. At that time, many conservationists were concerned that mountain gorillas would be extinct by the end of the twentieth century.

Then, in 2000, Amy Vedder returned to Karisoke and saw Pablo again. At twenty-six-years old, Pablo was the dominant silverback of his family. Silverbacks, named for the silver patches on their backs, are the largest adult male gorillas more than fifteen years of age in a family group. Pablo was responsible for the largest gorilla family ever seen: a family of forty-four.[4] The sight of Pablo and his family gave Vedder hope for the future.

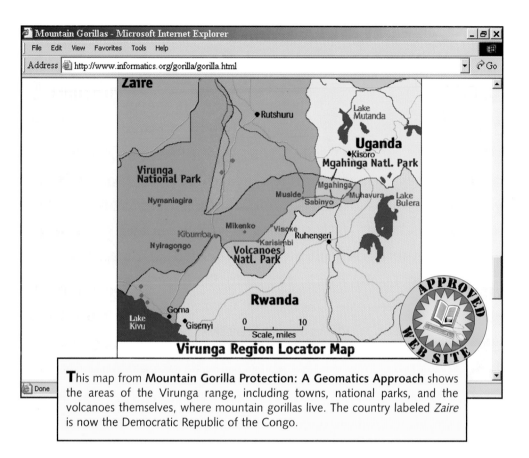

Mountain Gorillas - Microsoft Internet Explorer

File   Edit   View   Favorites   Tools   Help

Address http://www.informatics.org/gorilla/gorilla.html   Go

Virunga Region Locator Map

This map from **Mountain Gorilla Protection: A Geomatics Approach** shows the areas of the Virunga range, including towns, national parks, and the volcanoes themselves, where mountain gorillas live. The country labeled *Zaire* is now the Democratic Republic of the Congo.

▶ Where Mountain Gorillas Live

There are only about seven hundred mountain gorillas in the world, and they live in only two small areas in east-central Africa. The most recent count found 380 gorillas roaming through a mountain rain forest, at elevations of 10,000 feet (3,048 meters) or more, in the Virunga volcanic mountain range. The Virunga volcanoes run along the borders of Rwanda, the Democratic Republic of the Congo (DRC; also known as the Congo), and Uganda. Another 320 mountain gorillas live in the Bwindi Impenetrable National Park in Uganda.

Although mountain gorillas live close to the equator, their Virunga home is high in the mountains. Temperatures are cool and often drop below freezing at night with almost 100 percent humidity, which makes cool temperatures feel colder. With so much moisture and rich volcanic soil, green plants grow in abundance. The vegetation is so thick in many places that it is difficult to walk through it. Sometimes, machetes are required to cut paths through the tangle of underbrush. One gorilla researcher described the area as an "undergrowth of thistles, nettles, wild celery, and other herbs growing six feet high."[5]

▶ Gorilla History

No one knows how long mountain gorillas have lived in the Virunga volcanoes region. Most people outside of Africa did not even know that gorillas existed until the beginning of the twentieth century.

Scientists who study gorillas and other primates think that in prehistoric times, gorillas lived in the lowland rain forests of west-central Africa. As the gorilla population grew, some gorillas migrated eastward. Later, climate change brought colder, drier temperatures and eventually separated the rain forest into two unconnected areas. The eastern gorillas found themselves cut off from the western gorillas. Then about 400,000 years ago, the eastern gorillas split into two groups.[6] Those remaining at lower elevations became the gorillas known as eastern lowland gorillas or Grauer's gorillas. Another group must have crossed a great expanse of bleak lava fields to reach the forests on the slopes of the Virunga volcanoes. This group became the mountain gorillas.

Gorilla Species

Today, based on studies of gorilla DNA, most scientists separate gorillas into two species: the western gorilla and the eastern gorilla. Western gorillas are more numerous. Their population was estimated at the beginning of the twenty-first century to be about 100,000.[7]

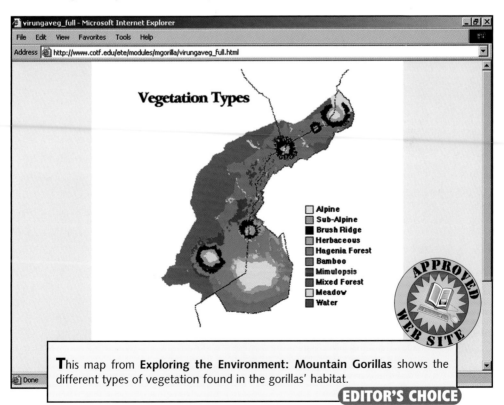

This map from **Exploring the Environment: Mountain Gorillas** shows the different types of vegetation found in the gorillas' habitat.

EDITOR'S CHOICE

▲ Mountain gorillas have longer faces and longer and darker hair than lowland gorillas.

Although western gorillas live in seven countries in Africa, their numbers are decreasing rapidly. They are losing their rain-forest habitat to development; they continue to be hunted; and disease, including the deadly Ebola virus, takes a toll.

Early in the twenty-first century, zoologists identified a subspecies of the western gorilla. This subspecies, called the Cross River gorilla, has a different skull and tooth size than other western gorillas. In 2005, conservationists counted only two hundred Cross River gorillas living in eight small groups along the border between Nigeria and Cameroon.[8]

Eastern gorillas are also divided into two subspecies. The eastern lowland gorillas, also known as Grauer's gorillas, live in the eastern part of the Congo. In 1998, the first attempt to count Grauer's gorillas revealed a population of about 17,000.[9] Civil war in the Congo has almost certainly caused that number to decrease because desperately hungry refugees, people driven from their homes and land by war, killed gorillas for food.

The other subspecies, mountain gorillas, live high in the Virunga volcano range, and although they are few in number, mountain gorillas are the most well known, since several mountain gorilla families have been studied on a daily basis for decades.

The eastern and western gorillas look very much alike. Generally, mountain gorillas are larger than other gorillas and have longer faces. Because mountain gorillas live in a cooler environment, their hair is longer, and it is jet black. The shorter hair of western gorillas is more likely to have a reddish tint.

All gorillas are hominids, members of the family Hominidae, which also includes orangutans, chimpanzees, and humans. Scientists studying the DNA of living apes as well as that of ancient fossils have developed a sort of family tree for members of the hominid family. According to estimates, orangutans were probably the first to become a separate branch of that tree, perhaps about 16 million years ago, although scientists disagree about the dates. A few million years later, gorillas and then chimpanzees became separate branches. As one gorilla researcher noted, "The startling conclusion is that gorillas and chimpanzees are more closely related to humans than either of them is to orangutans."[10]

▶ Discovery

Before the mid-1800s, almost no one outside the areas where gorillas live knew of their existence. Occasionally an explorer or adventurer would write of an animal larger than a chimpanzee, but the animal was never identified. Then in 1846, two missionaries found several gorilla skulls, which they sent to two well-known anatomy specialists.

In 1856, an American hunter killed a lowland gorilla in western Africa. His very dramatic account of his encounter with the gorilla exaggerated its ferociousness. In 1902 a German army officer was the first to shoot a mountain gorilla. Traveling through Rwanda, then a German colony, Captain Robert von Beringe decided to climb one of the Virunga volcanoes. Spotting a group of large, black apes, the captain shot two of them. He and the men accompanying him managed to retrieve one of the bodies from a ravine. Von Beringe sent the skeleton to a German scientist who declared the mountain gorilla to be a new species and named it *Gorilla gorilla beringei* in honor of the captain.

The discovery of a new species inspired hunters to travel great distances to kill the creatures no one knew

Mountain Gorilla, Article by Adrian Warren - page 3 of 6 - Microsoft Internet Explorer

File   Edit   View   Favorites   Tools   Help

Address http://www.lastrefuge.co.uk/data/articles/gorilla_p2_2.html   Go

©von Beringe

©von Beringe

Captain Robert von Beringe
(Courtesy von Beringe private
collection)

Captain Robert von Beringe
(Courtesy von Beringe private
collection)

"From October 16th. to 18th., senior physician Dr Engeland and I together with only a few Askaris and the

In 1902, the first documented discovery of a mountain gorilla was made by Captain Robert von Beringe, a German officer in what was then German East Africa. Von Beringe, whose pictures appear on the **Mountain Gorillas** Web site, described the animals he saw on the crest of Rwanda's Sabyinyo volcano as "big, black monkeys."

very much about. Between 1902 and 1925, hunters killed more than fifty mountain gorillas, in the name of science or for sport.[11] An American naturalist named Carl Akeley shot five gorillas for the American Museum of Natural History so that they could be studied and exhibited. However, Akeley was so impressed by these great apes that he decided he would rather study their lives than end them.

▶ Early Protection

After World War I, control of Rwanda passed to Belgium. Akeley persuaded Belgium's Prince Albert to establish the first national park in Africa in the Virunga volcanoes. The land was set aside for the protection and study of the gorillas. Akeley hoped to be the first to study the gorillas, and in 1926 he found a meadow named Kabara on the Congo side of the volcanoes. He built a cabin there to serve as his base, but he became ill and then died of malaria before he could begin his studies.

It would be another thirty years before a scientist ventured into the Virunga volcanoes to learn about the gorillas. In 1959, an American zoologist named George Schaller traveled to Kabara to observe the gorillas. During the months he spent watching them, he learned that they were not so ferocious after all. He wrote later, "In all the months I spent with the gorillas, none attacked me."[12]

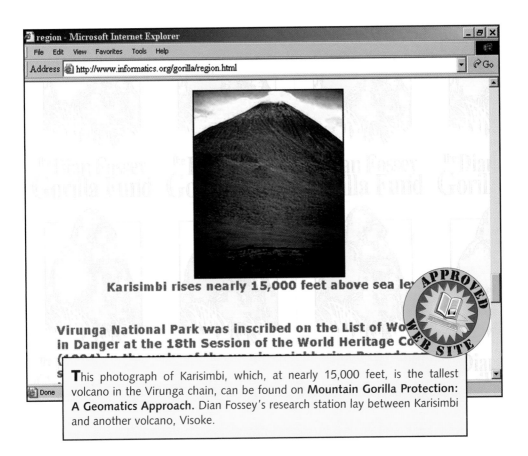

region - Microsoft Internet Explorer

File   Edit   View   Favorites   Tools   Help

Address http://www.informatics.org/gorilla/region.html   Go

Karisimbi rises nearly 15,000 feet above sea le

Virunga National Park was inscribed on the List of Wo in Danger at the 18th Session of the World Heritage Co

This photograph of Karisimbi, which, at nearly 15,000 feet, is the tallest volcano in the Virunga chain, can be found on **Mountain Gorilla Protection: A Geomatics Approach.** Dian Fossey's research station lay between Karisimbi and another volcano, Visoke.

▶ Fossey and Fame Come to the Gorillas

Schaller wrote two widely read books about his time spent with the gorillas. Among the people who read Schaller's books was a young occupational therapist named Dian Fossey. Though Fossey was then not a scientist, she was fascinated by the gorillas. She arrived at Kabara in 1967, intent on studying them. Six months later, a rebellion in the Congo forced her to move her research to Rwanda. In a high meadow between two volcanoes, she established a research station. The location was a saddle area, about ten thousand feet (three thousand meters) above sea level, between the Karisimbi and Visoke volcanoes. She borrowed from the names of the volcanoes to name her new camp "Karisoke." During the years that Fossey lived at Karisoke, a number of students came to work with her. Some of the individuals most active in gorilla conservation today first learned about gorillas at Karisoke.

Dian Fossey learned to modify her own behavior so that the gorillas would accept her and she could study them at close range. The family groups that Fossey studied were referred to simply as Group 4 and Group 5, but she did name individual gorillas, and these included Uncle Bert, Beethoven, Effie, and Marchessa. Most important for the conservation of mountain gorillas, Dian Fossey made the world aware of these gentle giants in the Virunga highlands. In the 1970s, people became fascinated by the lone American woman who lived with gorillas. Her photographs were printed in *National Geographic* magazine, and television crews made documentaries showing her in the midst of a gorilla family. People as far away as the United States could feel they knew the mountain gorilla family.

One of the gorillas the world came to know through Dian Fossey was Digit. After poachers killed Digit, thousands of people in the United States and England sent angry postcards to the government of Rwanda, where Digit's gorilla family lived. Fossey set up a fund known as the Digit Fund to finance antipoaching

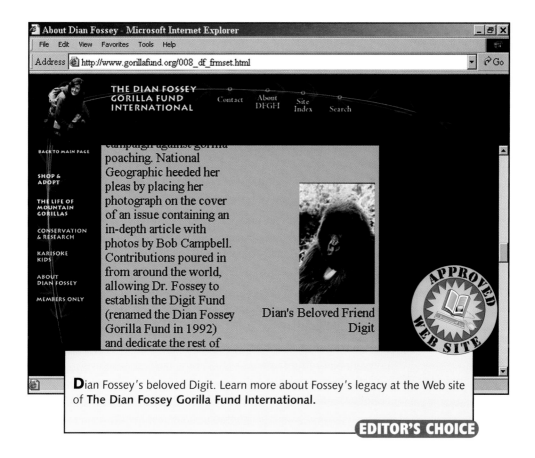

About Dian Fossey - Microsoft Internet Explorer

File   Edit   View   Favorites   Tools   Help

Address   http://www.gorillafund.org/008_df_frmset.html   Go

THE DIAN FOSSEY
GORILLA FUND
INTERNATIONAL

Contact   About DFGFI   Site Index   Search

BACK TO MAIN PAGE

SHOP & ADOPT

THE LIFE OF MOUNTAIN GORILLAS

CONSERVATION & RESEARCH

KARISOKE KIDS

ABOUT DIAN FOSSEY

MEMBERS ONLY

...campaign against gorilla poaching. National Geographic heeded her pleas by placing her photograph on the cover of an issue containing an in-depth article with photos by Bob Campbell. Contributions poured in from around the world, allowing Dr. Fossey to establish the Digit Fund (renamed the Dian Fossey Gorilla Fund in 1992) and dedicate the rest of

Dian's Beloved Friend
Digit

Dian Fossey's beloved Digit. Learn more about Fossey's legacy at the Web site of **The Dian Fossey Gorilla Fund International.**

EDITOR'S CHOICE

efforts. Thousands of dollars poured into conservation groups for programs to help save the mountain gorillas and preserve their habitat.

Gorilla Tourism

Beginning in 1979, one of the programs that money helped fund was gorilla tourism—bringing people to the areas where gorillas are so that tourist revenue helps save the animals. Since then, tourism has brought millions of dollars to Rwanda, the Congo, and Uganda. This money is tremendously important for gorilla conservation because many of the people living in the countries where the gorillas live are poor. People who struggle to feed themselves and their families have little energy left to care about the survival of an animal species like the mountain gorilla. But when the gorillas bring jobs and foreign dollars to the area, the animals become important to their host countries. Conservation organizations have recently concentrated on ways to ensure that tourism brings benefits to the people who live closest to the gorillas—as well as to the gorillas themselves.

Tragically, Dian Fossey was murdered at Karisoke in 1985, and the original Karisoke station was destroyed in 1994 following the Rwandan civil war. But scientists who studied with Fossey have carried on her campaign

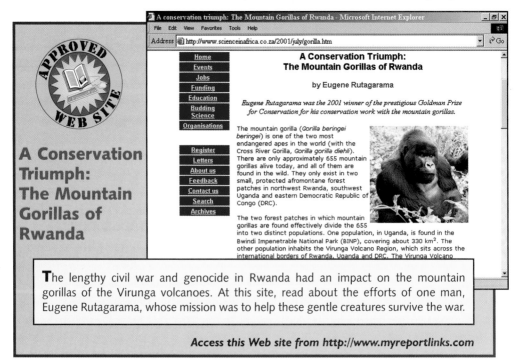

A Conservation Triumph: The Mountain Gorillas of Rwanda

The lengthy civil war and genocide in Rwanda had an impact on the mountain gorillas of the Virunga volcanoes. At this site, read about the efforts of one man, Eugene Rutagarama, whose mission was to help these gentle creatures survive the war.

Access this Web site from http://www.myreportlinks.com

to save the mountain gorillas. The Dian Fossey Gorilla Fund International (DFGFI), which began as the Digit Fund; the International Gorilla Conservation Programme (IGCP); and the Wildlife Conservation Society are actively involved in protecting the gorillas and their habitat. Extremely dedicated and courageous Rwandan, Congolese, and Ugandan park guards risk their lives—and sometimes lose them—to protect the mountain gorillas.

What You Can Do to Help Save Mountain Gorillas

Mountain gorillas live on another continent, thousands of miles from the United States, but the distance has not stopped people in the United States from helping the gorillas survive. Many Americans knew about Digit from magazine articles and television documentaries. When poachers killed Digit, people responded by sending postcards and letters to the Rwandan government. People who could give money sent contributions to conservation organizations to help protect gorillas and their habitat.

You are already taking the first step to act on behalf of the gorillas by learning about them. Once you are familiar with the facts, you can stay informed by watching for news articles about mountain gorillas and the countries they live in. For example, conservation organizations that work to protect gorillas often have news stories on their Web sites. Check these Web sites

Partners in Conservation - Microsoft Internet Explorer

File   Edit   View   Favorites   Tools   Help

Address http://www.colszoo.org/Conservation/pic/pic1.htm

Columbus ZOO and Aquarium

Visitor Information   Education/Groups
Calendar of Events   Membership
Support the Zoo   Conservation

Animal Areas

Select an area

Search   Go   Home | Contact Us | Press Room | Job Opportunities

Partners In Conservation

In 1991, staff and volunteers at the Columbus Zoo learned about the outbreak of civil war in Rwanda through magazines, newspapers and television accounts. They immediately thought about the safety of the gorillas, but were also numbed as they read about the suffering of the people of Rwanda.

Partners In Conservation or [PIC] was initiated in direct response to what was happening in Rwanda. Columbus Zoo Docents, Barb DeLorme, Judy Hoffman Bolton and Jeff Ramsey, met Gorilla Keeper, Charlene Jendry, one evening after work to determine if there was something they could do to help. At that meeting, they decided on a program name and mission statement. The goals have remained the

There are only 360 mountain gorillas left on earth; their habitats are in the Virunga Mountains of Rwanda and the

Partners In Conservation
Project Updates
Artisan Mechandise Brochure
You Can Help!
Frederic Ndabaramiye
How PIC Met Frederic Ndabaramiye
Frederic Update - July 2004
Donation

APPROVED WEB SITE

Staff at Ohio's Columbus Zoo formed the Partners in Conservation program to help both the people and mountain gorillas of central Africa. Read more about their global conservation efforts at the Web site of the **Columbus Zoo.**

often. Situations change continually, and those who want to save endangered species need to watch for changes that threaten them. War, famine, and disease among the people who live near the gorillas all affect the species' survival. Share what you learn with the adults around you. Discuss conservation problems to help them understand the needs of the mountain gorilla.

One adult you can talk to is your teacher. If your class or your school participates in fund-raising projects, find out about programs that might allow your group to "adopt a gorilla." The African Wildlife Foundation and the Dian Fossey Gorilla Fund International are two of the organizations that have adopt-a-gorilla programs. Talk to your teacher about the possibility of adopting a gorilla as a class project.

Visit a zoo close to you, and find out if the zoo is involved in protecting endangered species. You will not find mountain gorillas in a zoo. For reasons that scientists do not yet understand, mountain gorillas do not survive in captivity. Any gorillas you see in a zoo are lowland gorillas, but American zoos are involved in helping mountain gorillas.

▶ A Day at the Zoo Can Save a Gorilla's Life

The Columbus Zoo in Ohio, a "Partner in Conservation," helps the Dian Fossey Gorilla Fund International

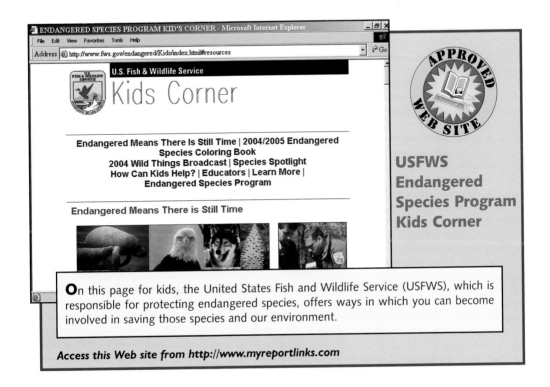

USFWS Endangered Species Program Kids Corner

On this page for kids, the United States Fish and Wildlife Service (USFWS), which is responsible for protecting endangered species, offers ways in which you can become involved in saving those species and our environment.

Access this Web site from http://www.myreportlinks.com

support the Karisoke Research Station, which is now in Ruhengeri, Rwanda. The Partners in Conservation program was begun by staff and docents (guides) with the Columbus Zoo who were concerned about the safety of the people and gorillas living in the areas affected by the civil war in Rwanda that began in 1991. The program helps raise awareness about the people and wildlife of Rwanda and the Congo and helps raise money for them from the sale of native crafts and fund-raising events. Each year, representatives from Partners in Conservation also visit Karisoke to see what is being done and what is needed for the future.

Other zoos participate in Partners in Conservation and provide volunteer assistance to mountain gorilla conservation. If there is a zoo close to you, find out if it is involved in efforts to save mountain gorillas. If it is not, you might talk to your teacher about beginning a class project that would influence that zoo to help mountain gorillas.

▶ Write to the People in Power

You might wonder what American politicians can do to help (or hurt) wildlife in another continent. The answer, in both cases, is "a lot." And although you can not yet vote, you can influence those who can.

One of the most important things you can do is persuade your parents and other voters to make sure that the Endangered Species Act of 1973, one of the most important conservation laws ever passed, is not weakened or repealed. If the United States is seen as being "soft" on environmental issues, other countries may follow suit. Know who your senators and congressional representatives are. Then, when you learn of a situation that affects endangered species, like the mountain gorillas of Virunga and Bwindi, write to tell your elected officials why it is important to save these animals. Get your friends and family members to write, too. You, just one person, can make a difference in whether mountain gorillas survive—or become lost to the world forever.

BEING A GORILLA

As dawn slowly changes the sky from black to gray, the gorillas begin to stir. The night before, they made bathtub-like nests of bent branches and leaves for protection from the cold. But the beginning of a new day means time for breakfast. The young gorillas, two to eight years old, are usually the first to get up in the cool morning air. While they wait for the adults to stir, they might play tag, wrestle, or climb a tree to swing from a branch.

Soon, the adults are up. The average gorilla family consists of about ten individuals: one or two mature males, several mature females, an infant or two, and several immature gorillas. One adult, usually the dominant silverback, will decide where the family should travel in search of food. The gorillas do not have far to go. They are surrounded by dense green vegetation, including wild celery, thistles, nettles, and other plants, that make up their diet.

▶ The Silverback

In the nineteenth century, Paul du Chaillu, an American explorer, described full-grown male gorillas as nightmarish creatures, terrible to behold. Although his accounts were considered too extreme by scientists, they were the most accurate descriptions of gorillas for many years.[1] The fear that male gorillas inspire is no accident. They are responsible for defending their families, so they need to be able to fight off predators. They also need to be stronger and braver than other male gorillas to attract and keep females.

In 1959 when George Schaller first saw a silverback mountain gorilla, he thought it was the "most magnificent animal" he had ever seen. He described the scene: "He lay on the slope, propped on his huge shaggy arms, and the muscles of his broad shoulders and silver back rippled. He gave an impression of dignity and

George Schaller described his first silverback as the "most magnificent animal" he had ever seen. This mountain gorilla sports the characteristic silver-streaked hair of the mature male.

Gorilla gorilla beringei

Access this Web site from http://www.myreportlinks.com

This University of Michigan Museum of Zoology site presents detailed information on mountain gorillas as part of its Animal Diversity Web database.

EDITOR'S CHOICE

restrained power, of absolute certainty in his majestic appearance."[2]

Male gorillas usually weigh from 300 to 400 pounds (140 to 180 kilograms). When they stand on their bowed legs, they are more than 5 feet 6 inches tall, and their arms may span 7 feet. In addition to size and strength, male gorillas are armed with strong jaws and large canine teeth. Supporting the jaw muscles is a crest of bone, called the sagittal crest, which runs along the top and back of their skulls.

Although a silverback gorilla has fearsome fighting ability, he would rather not fight at all. Usually, his first response is a bluff intended to strike fear into the heart of whatever threatens his family, whether the threat is from a leopard, another gorilla, or a poacher with a gun. To demonstrate his might, the silverback stands and screams a warning. The noise is impressive. George Schaller described a "tremendous roar [that] filled the chasm and bounding from wall to wall descended the mountain like the rumbling of an avalanche."[3] As he roars, the silverback beats his chest with his hands. The male gorilla's enormous chest is hairless, so there is nothing to deaden the sound. And inside his chest cavity, his voice box has extensions that form inflatable air pouches that make the hollow *poketa-poketa* sound louder. He might also show his strength by breaking branches or pulling small trees from the ground as he moves forward.

▶ "Stand Your Ground!"

One of the first lessons that gorilla researchers have to learn is to stand their ground when a silverback charges. The charge is almost always a bluff, and the gorilla will stop a few feet away to evaluate the person's reaction. Running invites a chase, which the gorilla will most likely win.

Dian Fossey admitted that she sometimes had to hold on to a tree to keep from running. Once, she took a tape recorder to capture the sounds gorillas make, called vocalizations. Several young gorillas watched her curiously and then began performing wild acrobatics in the trees. Soon their noise caught the attention of the adults who were munching on plants a little distance away. The adults, led by the silverback, charged.

When Fossey played the tape recording later, she heard her dramatic whisper, "I'll never get out of this alive!"[4] The tape recorder also provided evidence that each gorilla's scream is distinct: Gorillas can identify one another from miles away.

▶ Females

Female gorillas are much shorter than males and weigh only half as much. Adult males and adult females are

Female mountain gorillas, while much shorter and lighter than males, still cast an imposing impression.

also very different looking from one another. Female gorillas do not have the powerful jaw muscles that silverbacks use for fighting, so they do not have the males' helmet-shaped sagittal crest. Females are also coal-black from head to foot—they never develop the silver saddle that marks a full-grown male.

▷ Family Ranks

In gorilla families, each member seems to have a ranking. The dominant silverback is the most important. Usually if he wants to sit where another family member is sitting, the other gorilla will simply move. Other adult males usually have a higher ranking than females. Among the females, the rank seems to depend on how long the female has been in the family. Next in importance would most likely be the offspring of the dominant female. Females who join the family later may never earn respected positions within the family. However, researchers have seen in day-to-day interactions that dominance of one gorilla over another sometimes changes.

Researchers Amy Vedder and Bill Weber witnessed such a change. One afternoon during an especially heavy rain, Effie, the dominant female in Beethoven's harem, or group of females, ran for shelter beneath a fallen tree. Two of her offspring—and the two researchers—scrambled after her. The three gorillas and two humans huddled together under the wide branches as Beethoven sat in what the researchers call

A mountain gorilla group. Note the lighter hair of the baby clinging to its mother.

the "classic rainy weather position: arms folded, head tipped down." The rain was especially heavy, though, and Beethoven decided the fallen-tree shelter should be his. He loomed in front of Effie. But Effie stood her ground and cough-grunted her opinion that the shelter was hers. Beethoven moved on to find another shelter from the rain.[5]

Infant Gorillas

Female gorillas usually give birth about once every four years. The gestation period for gorillas, like humans, is about nine months. Infant gorillas weigh only 4 to 5 pounds (1.8 to 2.3 kilograms) when they are born.[6] Smaller than most human infants and almost as helpless, they are in constant contact with their mothers during the first months of their lives. When the mother walks, her baby clings to the hair on her chest or stomach. When the mother rests, she often cradles her baby in one arm.

At about six months of age, young gorillas begin to explore the world beyond their mothers, although their mothers keep a watchful eye on them. Their exploration includes the food their mothers eat. As mothers chomp on nettles and wild celery, bits and pieces of food fall on the young gorillas so that they can see what adults eat and sample pieces. Until they are about two and a half to three years old, young gorillas' primary food is their mothers' milk.

By the time young gorillas are a year old, they have progressed from clinging to their mother's stomach to riding on her back, jockey style. At about eighteen months, they move freely among family members and begin to play with other young gorillas. George Schaller estimated that young gorillas weigh fifteen to twenty pounds at age one, about sixty pounds at age three, and about one hundred and twenty pounds by the age of five.[7]

▶ Gorilla Play

Researchers Amy Vedder and Bill Weber noted that young gorillas spend about a third of their waking hours playing and their games are like the games that human children play. They noted that a fallen tree can be just right "for a rough-and-tumble version of king of the mountain, with the added complexity of a slippery trunk and dangling vines as alternate attack routes to the top."[8] Tag and wrestling are also favorite games of young mountain gorillas.

Young gorillas also involve their fathers in their play. Researchers often saw young gorillas chasing each other around and over their imposing, 350-pound silverback father. As one researcher observed, "It is not unusual to see an adult male surrounded by a cluster of infants and juveniles, with their mothers nowhere in sight, as if the silverback were a sort of day care center."[9]

Sometimes, the researchers themselves became "playmates," whether they wanted to or not. As Amy

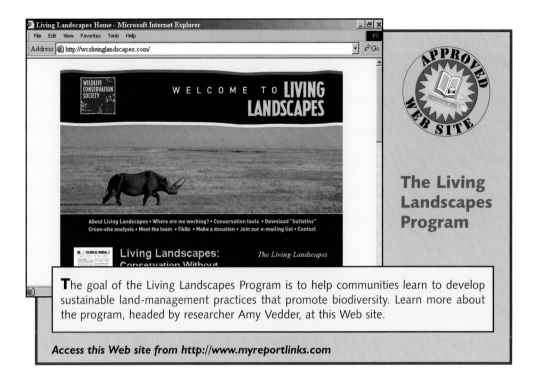

Living Landscapes Home - Microsoft Internet Explorer

File   Edit   View   Favorites   Tools   Help

Address | http://wcslivinglandscapes.com/   Go

WELCOME TO **LIVING LANDSCAPES**

WILDLIFE
CONSERVATION
SOCIETY

About Living Landscapes • Where are we working? • Conservation tools • Download "bulletins"
Cross-site analysis • Meet the team • FAQs • Make a donation • Join our e-mailing list • Contact

Living Landscapes:
Conservation Without   *The Living Landscapes*

The Living Landscapes Program

The goal of the Living Landscapes Program is to help communities learn to develop sustainable land-management practices that promote biodiversity. Learn more about the program, headed by researcher Amy Vedder, at this Web site.

Access this Web site from http://www.myreportlinks.com

Vedder sat quietly one day, two young gorillas began to circle her, chasing each other. Soon they added to the game by dragging vines with them. By the time the gorillas lost interest because there were no more vines handy, Vedder had become so tightly entangled that she had to use a knife to free herself.[10]

▶ Adolescence

When gorillas are about six years old, they are considered adolescents. Young males begin to grow faster than young females. By the age of eight or nine, the males, known as black backs, are much larger than females of the same age. Black-back gorillas develop the high crest that supports their stronger jaw muscles.

Mountain gorilla families are close-knit groups and may number up to thirty members.

When black backs are about thirteen years old, the hair on their backs begins to turn silver, and they are called silverbacks. Females are usually mature by the age of eight or nine.

As the young male gorillas mature, they often leave their families. The process may take several years as they spend more and more time at the outer edge of the group, doing sentry duty and getting used to being on their own. Eventually they leave the family and wander off to find females and start their own families. Starting a family may take a few more years, though, and single males sometimes travel together for company. Some males never leave the family, however, and are able to take on the responsibilities of a dominant silverback when it dies.

Young females do not go off on their own. When it is time for them to leave their families, they join another family or a single male.

▶ Foraging for Food

Adult mountain gorillas spend most of their waking hours eating. Because they live high in the mountain rain forest, most of what they eat is green foliage, such as wild celery, thistles, and nettles. Thistles and nettles are both difficult to eat because of their sharp spikes and stinging leaves. To eat thistles, the gorillas use their nimble hands to fold the spiky outside of the leaf into the center and carefully place the folded leaf packet into the side of their mouth. They pick nettles by sliding

▲ *A flowering plant provides a tasty morsel for this young mountain gorilla. While plants are abundant in the gorillas' habitat, the animals must eat a lot of them to get enough nourishment.*

two fingers up the stem from underneath to push the stinging side of the leaves together. Both plants are worth the effort, though, because they are high in nutrition.

Blackberries are a favorite food when gorillas can find them. Another favorite food is bracket fungus, which grows shelflike on trees. Of all the plants that gorillas eat, young bamboo shoots provide the most protein. These shoots are available five months of the year at the lower elevations of their habitat. Gorillas search for the three- to four-foot shoots and peel away their thin covering to eat the juicy core.

During the dry months, gorillas will sometimes make long trips to specific sites where they eat dirt—but not any old dirt. Researchers have examined this dirt and found it high in potassium and other minerals that are good for the gorillas.

▶ Salad to Go

What gorillas eat depends partly on what is available where they are. When George Schaller observed the mountain gorillas in Uganda's Bwindi Impenetrable Forest, he identified twenty-seven plants included in their diet. Only nine of those plants are also found in the Virunga volcanoes region. When Amy Vedder studied the diet of the Virunga mountain gorillas, she found that their diet was extremely varied—they ate more than one hundred kinds of foods, and all were high in nutrition.[11]

Since gorillas are surrounded by the food they eat, they do not usually need to travel far on any day. A mountain gorilla family's home range is usually only 3 to 5 square miles (8 to 13 square kilometers), although gorillas might travel beyond their usual territory to find a specific food at a certain time of year.

▲ *This gorilla group settles down for a snug nap in their day nest.*

The advantage of living on the green plants growing all around them is that there is always plenty to eat. The disadvantage is that the gorillas have to eat a lot to get the nutrition they need. A silverback may eat 40 to 50 pounds (18 to 23 kilograms) of greenery in a

▲ The long, thick hair of mountain gorillas makes grooming an important ritual.

day. The large quantities of roughage they eat are what give them their potbellies.

With so much food around them, mountain gorillas do not have to compete to get enough to eat. But they do sometimes fight over particularly tasty food. When

they are eating, they often fan out so that they may not even see one another in the dense foliage. Sometimes two gorillas spot the same piece of choice food. Researcher Amy Vedder, who spent more than two thousand hours analyzing the foods that one gorilla family ate, wrote that nothing prepared her for the "sudden outbreaks of intense, almost maniacal screaming" when two gorillas want the same bit of food.[12] The screaming usually lasts for only a matter of seconds. Sometimes the silverback ends an especially noisy disagreement by taking the food being fought over for himself. While screaming matches are common, physical violence within a gorilla family is rare.

Close-knit Families

In fact, gorilla families are very close. Their social behavior is most evident during their midday rest periods when the gorillas stop eating to digest their food. For the young gorillas, "rest" periods begin with a time of intense playing. Adults often take time to groom each other, pulling twigs, leaves, or insects from the thick, 4- to 6-inch-long (10- to 15-centimeter-long) hair of the other gorilla. When the gorillas finally settle down to sleep in day nests, they often maintain some physical contact.

Researchers observing gorillas have often noted what seem to be displays of affection, especially between the silverback and other family members. George Schaller's earliest glimpses into gorilla life included one such display. As he watched from some distance away, a female with a newborn approached the silverback and leaned against him. The silverback reached over and caressed the tiny infant.[13]

Dian Fossey observed another silverback watching a six-month-old infant "tadpoling" across its mother's stomach. The silverback picked up the little gorilla to groom it before returning it to its mother.[14] If a young gorilla is orphaned before it is old enough to care for itself, it is often the silverback—not one of the other females—that adopts the orphan, sharing its night nest to keep the small gorilla warm and protecting it in family squabbles.

Some scientists think that gorilla families stay together because food is abundant and there is no need to separate to search for it. George Schaller expressed the opinion that gorilla families might just stay together because they like each other. Several

Gorilla Tool Kit - Microsoft Internet Explorer

File   Edit   View   Favorites   Tools   Help

Address   http://www.wcs.org/353624/gorillatoolkit

Our Mission   Around the Globe   WCS in New York   High-Tech Tools   Education   Search   Home

WILDLIFE CONSERVATION SOCIETY

SAVING WILDLIFE

VISIT OUR PARKS >>   BRONX ZOO   NEW YORK AQUARIUM   CENTRAL PARK ZOO   QUEENS ZOO   PROSPECT PARK ZOO

Gorilla Tool Kit

Back to Previous Page

Before the advent of ape powertools, our closest ancestors discovered termite fishing-sticks and stone-nutcrackers. Now, gorillas have proven they are just a few steps away from the depth gauge and the trekking pole. According to a study by the Wildlife Conservation Society (WCS) and other organizations, for the first time scientists have observed and photographed wild gorillas using tools. Up to four other species of great apes, including chimpanzees and orangutans, have been observed using tools in the wild, but not gorillas.

Researchers with the **Wildlife Conservation Society,** working in the rain forests of the Republic of Congo, have recently made a landmark discovery: They have seen gorillas in the wild using tools. Learn more about the work of this organization at its Web site.

EDITOR'S CHOICE

APPROVED WEB SITE

researchers have noted that when one gorilla family member is sick, the others travel shorter distances and wait for the slower member to catch up.

Gorilla Talk

Every day as the gorillas fan out to eat, they maintain contact with a sound that Dian Fossey called "belch vocalizations." The purpose of these purring noises seems to be to communicate "I'm here, and everything is fine." As one gorilla vocalizes, others answer. Gorillas often make these sounds as they are preparing to move on after resting, as if to make sure everyone agrees.

Gorillas use a sharp, harsh grunt to indicate displeasure. Dian Fossey called this sound a "pig grunt." Other researchers referred to it as a "cough grunt." The meaning was never in doubt, though. It is a warning to other gorillas to stop doing whatever they are doing.

Researchers including Amy Vedder sometimes heard the Group 5 gorillas singing, usually when the gorillas were in the midst of especially good food. As Vedder described this, "One individual would start a low rumbling sound, breathing loudly in and out in a modulated tone." Other gorillas would join in, each adding its distinctive sound, until, according to Vedder, "The result was a chorus of intertwined melodies, rising and falling in a natural rhythm that might continue for several minutes: a gorilla Gregorian chant in the Virunga cathedral."[15]

▷ Transfers

As young females become adults, they usually leave their families. Sometimes an older female who has no status in the family may choose to leave and join a smaller family. Females leave only when they can immediately join another family or a single male.

Meetings of two gorilla families seem to be accidental. While gorillas have a home territory where they spend most of their time, their territories are not well defined or well protected. Because the territories overlap and because gorilla families occasionally journey outside their home territory, two families do sometimes meet—and "the show" begins!

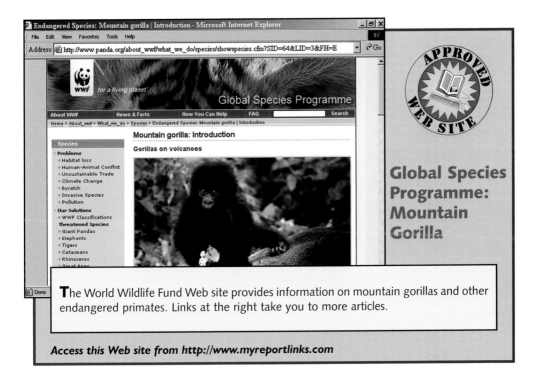

Global Species Programme: Mountain Gorilla

The World Wildlife Fund Web site provides information on mountain gorillas and other endangered primates. Links at the right take you to more articles.

Access this Web site from http://www.myreportlinks.com

▶ Exciting Get-togethers

Encounters between mountain gorilla families are often dramatic events as the males show off their strength, hoping to attract females from the other family. Dian Fossey described one such encounter between Beethoven, the mature leader of Group 5, and Uncle Bert, a much younger silverback who had recently taken charge of Group 4.

The interaction between the families extended from one day to the next. Uncle Bert, still young and needing to prove himself, began by putting on a great display. He strutted, his forearms stiff and taut, and broke tree branches with a snap. Then he stood to scream and beat his broad chest. Beethoven ignored him.

Meanwhile, several young gorillas in Beethoven's Group 5 scampered across the ravine to play with the young gorillas in Group 4. The adult females in Group 5 were as calm as their leader, but the Group 4 gorillas were excited by their leader's dramatic displays. Eventually, Uncle Bert strutted into the ravine, followed by several members of his family, as well as the young Group 5 gorillas that had come to visit. Leaving his family on the ridge, Beethoven strutted into the ravine to meet the other silverback.

According to Fossey, Uncle Bert and Beethoven approached each other, stopping within four feet, and stood rigid, neither looking at the other.[16] (Gorillas seem to think that staring is the height of rudeness. They quickly look away if another gorilla—or a human researcher—returns their gaze.) The other gorillas were silent, watching the drama. Suddenly, Uncle Bert beat his chest and smacked the foliage. Beethoven charged—and Uncle Bert turned and fled, followed by his family.

As night approached, Beethoven herded his playful young family members back to the group. That night, both families slept peacefully on different sides of the ravine. The next day, the young gorillas again played together as the males repeated their displays. Again Beethoven herded his family together as the group headed off.

No females migrated to the other family during that particular incident, but such meetings provide opportunities for the young gorillas to transfer. And not all such encounters are as bloodless. Severe bite wounds may result, and silverback gorillas sometimes die from their wounds.

Life Span

About two of every five infant gorillas die during their first year. Some of the deaths are caused by unrelated silverbacks. Causes of other infant deaths are not known.

Wild gorillas that make it past infancy may live for twenty-five to thirty years but not much more.[17] Adult gorillas who have lived past age thirty-five are considered elderly.

THREATS

As the world's human population continues to grow and take over lands that once provided animals with habitat, more and more animal species face extinction. Loss of habitat is the greatest threat to the survival of most animals species—and that includes the mountain gorillas.

Mountain gorillas live in only a small part of east-central Africa, in a mountainous region known as

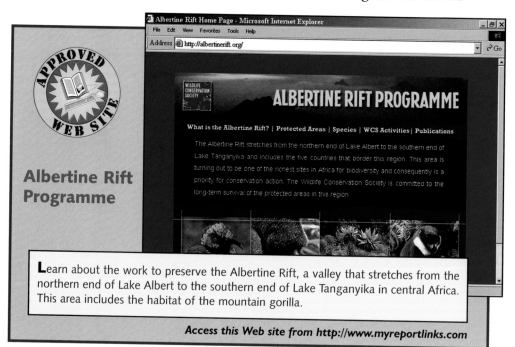

Albertine Rift Programme

Learn about the work to preserve the Albertine Rift, a valley that stretches from the northern end of Lake Albert to the southern end of Lake Tanganyika in central Africa. This area includes the habitat of the mountain gorilla.

Access this Web site from http://www.myreportlinks.com

the African lake district. Here a deep valley, about thirty miles (fifty kilometers) wide, is known as the Central Albertine Rift or the Western Rift Valley. From the floor of the valley, where the borders of the Congo, Rwanda, and Uganda meet, rise the eight Virunga volcanoes. The highest peak is Karisimbi, which rises to an elevation of 14,787 feet (4,507 meters). Two of the volcanoes, Nyamlagira and Nyiragongo, are still active. Although it is the smallest of the volcanoes at 10,049 feet (3,063 meters), Nyamlagira erupted a number of times in the 1980s and 1990s. Nyiragongo erupted in 1949, 1997, 2002, and 2004. The 2002 eruption was devastating: It destroyed a large portion of the Congolese city of Goma and killed hundreds of people.

▷ Mountain and Forest

Where the volcanoes' mountainsides are not covered by lava, they support a dense rain-forest habitat. Although the high elevations mean that temperatures often drop below freezing at night, a variety of trees and plants flourish in the rich volcanic soil. Rain is almost constant for several months of the year. The long rainy season begins in mid-February. In April and May, heavy downpours often continue all day and all night, dumping several inches of rain within twenty-four hours. By June the rains taper off, and July and August are almost totally dry. From the months of September through early December, rainfall becomes more frequent until January, which is usually a relatively dry month.

Africa's First National Park

As late as the early 1800s, the mountain gorillas' habitat stretched for hundreds of miles across the mountainous area from Rwanda and neighboring Congo north into Uganda. By the middle of the 1800s, farmers began to clear land in the lower elevations in Uganda. Eventually the gorillas' habitat was split into two separate chunks: Uganda's Impenetrable Forest and the Virunga volcanoes. The Virunga gorillas and the gorillas of the Impenetrable Forest now have no contact with each other.

By the 1920s, when Carl Akeley became interested in saving the gorillas, Belgium ruled Rwanda and the Congo. Akeley persuaded Belgium's Prince Albert to preserve the Virunga volcano area for the gorillas. In 1925, Prince Albert established Albert National Park,

Forest Conservation Portal

Access this Web site from http://www.myreportlinks.com

Loss of habitat is one of the greatest threats to endangered species. The Forest Conservation Portal is maintained by Forests.org, an international organization that works to conserve forests around the world. This educational site includes an archive of forest conservation news.

which was Africa's first national park, in Rwanda. In 1929 the park was expanded into the Congo, and it eventually covered 4,000 square miles (10,360 square kilometers).[1] In 1930 the Impenetrable Forest was set aside as a gorilla sanctuary, and it was designated as a forest reserve in 1939. It is now part of the Bwindi Impenetrable National Park.

▷ Diminishing Habitat

Since the early 1900s, the human population of the area has grown dramatically. About 90 percent of the people there still survive by subsistence farming, which means they struggle to grow just enough to live on.[2] Rwanda, for example, is slightly smaller than the state of Maryland, but its population in 2005 was estimated at 8.4 million.[3] With so many people trying to grow enough food to survive, land is precious.

As the population increased during the 1900s, farmers began clearing the forested parkland along the lower elevations of the Virunga volcanoes and the Impenetrable Forest. Cattle were herded into the parks to graze in the meadows. To provide meat for their families, both farmers and cattle herders hunted in the forest and set traps for small antelope. They also took wood from the forest to build fires. In 1950, people were allowed to farm the lower elevations of the Impenetrable Forest, which meant the gorillas had to live at elevations above 9,000 feet. In 1958 the Belgians, who still ruled Rwanda and the Congo, allowed 20,000 acres (8,094 hectares) of the Virunga parkland in Rwanda to be cleared for farming. That forced the gorillas to move higher into the mountainous region of that park, too.

▷ More Habitat Loss

During the 1960s, Rwanda, Uganda, and the Congo became independent countries, and each country became responsible for its portion of the gorillas' habitat. The Albert National Park became the Parc National des Volcans (Volcanoes National Park) in Rwanda, the

http://www.nasa.gov/centers/goddard/images/content/104882main_gorilla-pic4-high.jpg - Microsoft Interne...

File   Edit   View   Favorites   Tools   Help

Address http://www.nasa.gov/centers/goddard/images/content/104882main_gorilla-pic4-high.jpg

Done

Deforestation remains a problem even in the protected park areas where mountain gorillas live. In this NASA image, the greener areas lie outside the boundaries of the Volcanoes National Park in Rwanda, while the brown areas, with burning vegetation, are inside Virunga National Park in the Congo. This image is found on NASA's **Gorillas in the Midst of Extinction** site.

Parc National des Virunga (Virunga National Park) in the Democratic Republic of the Congo, and the Mgahinga Gorilla National Park in Uganda.

In 1969, the Rwandan government saw an opportunity to make money by growing pyrethrum, a natural insecticide. When the chemical insecticide DDT was banned in Western countries because it was found to be toxic to many animals, pyrethrum, which grows only at high altitudes, was suddenly in demand. Another 25,000 acres (10,118 hectares) of the Parc National des Volcans became farmland for growing pyrethrum. The market for pyrethrum soon ended as scientists developed synthetic insecticides, but farmers remained at the edge of a smaller gorilla habitat.

Moving Up

As the lower elevations of the gorillas' habitat disappeared, the gorillas simply moved higher. Even though mountain gorillas are adapted to living at higher elevations, the cold, humid climate of their habitat makes them vulnerable to pneumonia. Newborns, weighing only about three pounds (one kilogram) at birth, are especially vulnerable. Pneumonia may be one reason that approximately two of every five infant gorillas die in their first year.

Loss of the lower elevations of the gorillas' habitat also reduced the supply of an important gorilla food: bamboo. Bamboo provides gorillas with their best source of protein.[4] But the lower elevations of the park

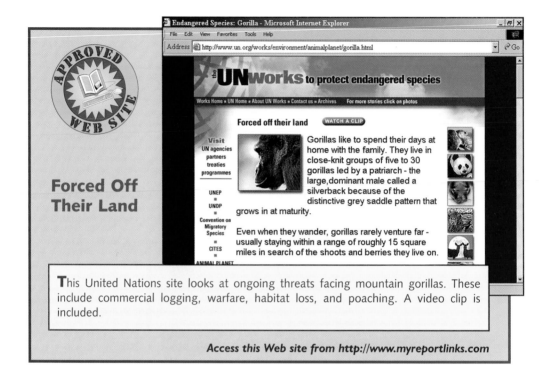

Endangered Species: Gorilla - Microsoft Internet Explorer

File   Edit   View   Favorites   Tools   Help

Address http://www.un.org/works/environment/animalplanet/gorilla.html   Go

the**UN**works to protect endangered species

Works Home ▪ UN Home ▪ About UN Works ▪ Contact us ▪ Archives   For more stories click on photos

Forced off their land   WATCH A CLIP

Visit
UN agencies
partners
treaties
programmes

UNEP
▪
UNDP
▪
Convention on
Migratory
Species
▪
CITES
▪
ANIMAL PLANET

Gorillas like to spend their days at home with the family. They live in close-knit groups of five to 30 gorillas led by a patriarch - the large, dominant male called a silverback because of the distinctive grey saddle pattern that grows in at maturity.

Even when they wander, gorillas rarely venture far - usually staying within a range of roughly 15 square miles in search of the shoots and berries they live on.

Forced Off Their Land

This United Nations site looks at ongoing threats facing mountain gorillas. These include commercial logging, warfare, habitat loss, and poaching. A video clip is included.

Access this Web site from http://www.myreportlinks.com

where bamboo once grew have been converted to farmland, and local people have found many uses for the remaining bamboo. It is used as a building material and is also used to make spring traps. Some gorilla groups never eat bamboo shoots, though, which shows that as nutritious as bamboo is, it is not necessary for gorilla survival.

In 1979, the Rwandan government considered taking another large chunk of the park—12,500 acres (5,059 hectares)—to raise cattle.[5] Conservationists successfully convinced the government that the gorillas could be worth more than cattle if they were part of a successful tourism project. Eventually the gorillas brought millions of dollars to Rwanda, the Congo, and Uganda.

The Ravages of War

But the affairs of the region's people continued to affect the gorillas and their habitat. Rwanda's Hutu people, the majority, were mainly farmers. Its Tutsi people, although a minority, were cattle owners and generally more prosperous. Intermarriage between the groups over the years and a common language and culture did not completely erase earlier differences, however. In 1990, a rebellion erupted in Rwanda with attacks on the Hutu-controlled Rwandan government by a rebel group of Tutsis that had been living in exile in

Frontline: Ghosts of Rwanda

This PBS site, a companion to a *Frontline* documentary, examines the mass killings in Rwanda in 1994 that were largely ignored by the Western world.

Access this Web site from http://www.myreportlinks.com

Uganda. Most of the rebels operated from the gorilla's home in the Virunga volcanoes. Although a peace agreement was signed in 1993, Rwanda's president was killed in 1994 when his airplane was shot down, and Hutu extremists in the Rwandan government began a campaign against the Tutsis. The killing of large groups of people ripped apart the fabric of Rwandan life. Within just a few months in 1994, the population of Rwanda went from about 7.6 million to about 4.8 million.[6] About eight hundred thousand Rwandans, mostly Tutsis, were killed. Great waves of refugees, about 2 million in all, fled Rwanda to nearby countries.[7]

Incredibly, both sides in the Rwandan civil war declared in 1990 that everything would be done to protect the mountain gorilla. That promise was especially significant because the rebel fighters had begun their operations from the gorillas' homeland. By the end of the conflict, only one gorilla was known to have been killed in Rwanda as a result of the fighting.[8]

▶ A Conflict Spreads

However, almost a million Rwandan refugees fled to the lower elevations of Virunga National Park in what was then Zaire (now the Democratic Republic of the Congo), where they struggled to find food. In 1994, the United Nations Educational, Scientific and Cultural Organization's World Heritage Committee added the Virunga National Park to its list of World Heritage in Danger because of damage to the park done by the refugees. The committee estimated that the refugees required about seven hundred tons (six hundred metric tons) of wood per day.[9]

Rwanda's civil war soon spilled into neighboring countries. In Zaire, which became the Democratic Republic of the Congo in 1997, unrest and frequent fighting continued for almost a decade. The result was

▲ For people living off the land in rural Africa, life is difficult. Learning to share that land with mountain gorillas and other wildlife has not always been easy.

that more than 2.5 million people died from combat, disease, or malnutrition. The civil war in the Congo soon involved other countries, including Rwanda and Uganda. The war also resulted in the deaths of at least sixteen mountain gorillas in the Congolese sector of the Virungas.[10]

In the spring of 2004, Rwandans crossed the border into the Democratic Republic of the Congo's Virunga National Park to clear land and farm it. By June they had cleared almost 6 square miles (15 square kilometers) of land at the park's lower elevation. Conservation organizations and Western governments put pressure on the Rwandan government to stop the destruction of the rain forest, and the farmers were driven out. In July, conservationists began building a three-foot-high

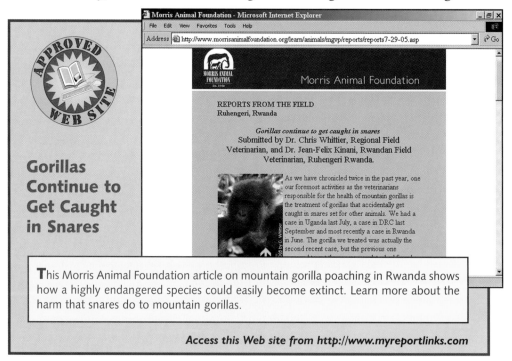

Gorillas Continue to Get Caught in Snares

Morris Animal Foundation - Microsoft Internet Explorer

File   Edit   View   Favorites   Tools   Help

Address   http://www.morrisanimalfoundation.org/learn/animals/mgvp/reports/reports7-29-05.asp

Morris Animal Foundation

REPORTS FROM THE FIELD
Ruhengeri, Rwanda

Gorillas continue to get caught in snares
Submitted by Dr. Chris Whittier, Regional Field Veterinarian, and Dr. Jean-Felix Kinani, Rwandan Field Veterinarian, Ruhengeri Rwanda.

As we have chronicled twice in the past year, one our foremost activities as the veterinarians responsible for the health of mountain gorillas is the treatment of gorillas that accidentally get caught in snares set for other animals. We had a case in Uganda last July, a case in DRC last September and most recently a case in Rwanda in June. The gorilla we treated was actually the second recent case, but the previous one

This Morris Animal Foundation article on mountain gorilla poaching in Rwanda shows how a highly endangered species could easily become extinct. Learn more about the harm that snares do to mountain gorillas.

Access this Web site from http://www.myreportlinks.com

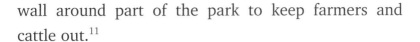

wall around part of the park to keep farmers and cattle out.[11]

▶ Poaching

Early in the 1900s, European and American hunters and scientists killed more than fifty mountain gorillas. Carl Akeley, an American naturalist, brought that killing to an end. However, gorillas were hunted again in the 1960s and 1970s when local people found a market among foreigners for the heads and hands of gorillas. Mountain gorillas are sometimes killed when poachers attempt to capture young gorillas for sale to zoos or as pets, although no mountain gorillas have ever survived in captivity. Two Rwandan gorillas were killed and a baby gorilla disappeared in 2002. Two people were arrested following the killings, the first poaching incident of this type in seventeen years, but the missing infant was not recovered.

In an area where people hunt animals of the forest for food, gorillas are often accidental victims. Poachers place traps to catch duiker or wild pigs. The traps are made by bending a sapling or a bamboo stem and attaching it to a wire noose. A peg attached to a horizontal stick holds the sapling in place until something steps in the noose's circle and depresses the stick. Instantly the sapling springs up, catching the leg of the animal in the noose.

Gorillas sometimes step into these snares. Adult gorillas can tear themselves free, although they may lose fingers or toes in the process. When the wire stays imbedded in a gorilla's wrist or leg, it can cause an infection that ultimately kills the animal.

Disease

Gorillas share a common ancestry with humans, and they are susceptible to the same diseases that people are. In their wet, cold habitat, mountain gorillas can easily be stricken by pneumonia. They are also known to have died from malaria, transmitted by mosquitoes. The Ebola virus, which is an especially fast-acting and deadly virus, has killed western gorillas. Even diseases that are not especially threatening to humans can be fatal to gorillas if the animals have not developed immunity to the diseases.

The tourism program that was developed to save mountain gorillas brings with it the threat of introducing new diseases that could wipe out entire gorilla families. Responsible tourism programs include measures to prevent physical contact between tourists and gorillas to avoid the spread of disease.

Chapter 4

"NO ONE LOVED GORILLAS MORE"

That mountain gorillas still survive is largely due to the work of one person: Dian Fossey. Fossey lived among the mountain gorillas of the Virungas for more than fifteen years. During those years she learned how to be accepted by these animals so that she could study them. She established the Karisoke Research Station, which, although now in a different location, continues to serve as a base for conservationists studying mountain gorillas. Fossey wrote detailed notes describing all that she learned about the gorillas in her many hours with them. Perhaps most importantly, as George Schaller wrote, "The mountain gorilla might have vanished quietly among its fog-shrouded peaks had not Dian Fossey and her coworkers remained as a determined presence, harrying poachers, confiscating snares, and, most importantly, drawing the attention of Rwanda's government as well as that of the international conservation community to the gorilla's plight."[1] Money raised by Western conservation groups still funds programs to help the gorillas survive.

▶ Fascinated by Gorillas

Dian Fossey began her work with limited scientific training. In the early 1960s, she was an occupational

This mountain gorilla might not be alive today if Dian Fossey had not made the world aware of the species' plight more than thirty years ago.

therapist in Louisville, Kentucky, who had a dream of going to Africa. One day she decided that "dreams seldom materialize on their own," so she went to a bank and took out a loan.[2] Then she spent months planning her seven-week "safari." The Internet was decades away; Fossey made all of her arrangements by writing letters.

When Fossey finally boarded a plane for Africa in September 1963, two goals at the top of her to-do list were to meet a well-known anthropologist named Louis Leakey and to see the mountain gorillas. Her meeting with Dr. Leakey was certainly memorable— she fell into his newest excavation in Tanzania and injured her ankle. Two weeks later, in spite of the painful ankle, the determined young woman limped up the steep path into the Virunga volcanoes to meet the gorillas. She watched them from fifty feet away, peering through the dense rain-forest undergrowth at leathery black faces peeking through the greenery at her. She left determined to return one day.

▶ Passing the Test

Dr. Leakey was also interested in the mountain gorillas. He hoped someone would want to study the gorillas in the way that Jane Goodall was then studying chimpanzees. Dr. Goodall, a leading primatologist, worked with Dr. Leakey for many years, studying the chimpanzees of Kenya before beginning her own research in Tanzania. Although Leakey's meeting with

Dian Fossey was very brief, he believed she was that person.

Three years after Leakey and Fossey met, Leakey traveled to Louisville, Kentucky, on a speaking tour and met with Fossey to suggest that she study gorillas. When she agreed, he began raising funds for the study—and Fossey had her appendix removed. The anthropologist had told her the surgery was necessary before she could live in the remote Virunga highlands. When Fossey came home from the hospital, she found a letter from Leakey. In it, he confessed that her surgery had not really been necessary—it was just his way of testing her determination.[3]

▶ The Adventure Begins

In December 1966, Dian Fossey once again boarded a plane for Africa. After she arrived, two British photographers who had spent some time in the Virungas gave her a crash course in camp life, although they were convinced that what the brand-new gorilla researcher planned to do was impossible. Fossey also spent two days with Jane Goodall at her chimpanzee research center. That was the extent of Fossey's training.

Fossey set up camp in the Kabara meadow on the slopes of Mount Mikeno in Zaire, where George Schaller had set up camp several years earlier. Then, with the help of a tracker, she began to learn about gorillas.

Studying gorillas required getting close enough to watch them without making them so nervous that they

Dian Fossey's first glimpse of mountain gorillas through the dense foliage of the African forest led her to vow to return.

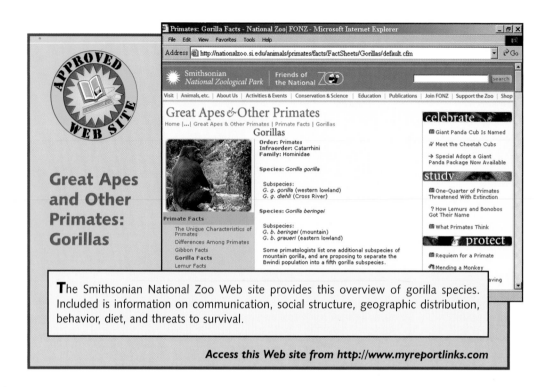

The Smithsonian National Zoo Web site provides this overview of gorilla species. Included is information on communication, social structure, geographic distribution, behavior, diet, and threats to survival.

Access this Web site from http://www.myreportlinks.com

would not behave normally. As Fossey tried different methods of making the gorillas comfortable with her, or habituating them, she realized that their curiosity would be a great help in the process.

Learning About Gorillas

One day, the researcher decided to climb a tree to take a picture of the gorillas. As she later wrote, tree climbing was not one of her better talents, and the tree was particularly "slithery." After much huffing, puffing, and branch breaking, Fossey had made little progress. The tracker who was with her gave her a boost, and she managed to pull herself to a height of about twenty feet (six meters). Feeling certain that all the noise of her clumsy tree-climbing efforts must have frightened the gorillas away, Fossey looked out from her perch to find "the entire group . . . sitting like front-row spectators at a sideshow."[4] Their curiosity was stronger than their fear.

Eventually she learned that her upright walking made the gorillas nervous. They were more comfortable if she "walked" on her knees and knuckles, the way that gorillas walk, or sat and pretended to eat the food they ate. And she continued to take advantage of the gorillas' curiosity. She put herself in plain view and let them come to her.

Fossey also tried imitating the gorillas' chest beats by slapping her thighs. The sound did get the gorillas' attention, but she later realized that she was sending the wrong message. Among gorillas, chest beating signals alarm or excitement. Instead, Fossey learned to imitate what she called a belch vocalization—"soft purring sounds resembling stomach rumbling"—that the gorillas used among themselves to communicate contentment.[5] She noticed that when one gorilla made the *naoom, naoom* stomach-rumbling sound, other gorillas answered with a similar sound. She interpreted the sound as one that announced the gorilla's presence and meant that everything was fine.

▶ A New Start

Suddenly the affairs of humans interrupted Fossey's work with the gorillas just six months after it had begun.

▲ Dian Fossey and one of the gorillas she studied at Karisoke. Fossey became a celebrity in 1970 when her photograph, with her gorillas, graced the cover of National Geographic magazine. This photograph was taken nine months later.

Armed soldiers informed her that there was a rebellion in progress and escorted her down the mountain.

Dian Fossey was nothing if not determined. Within a few months, she was again setting up camp in the Virunga volcanoes, this time in Rwanda's Parc National des Volcans, in a camp she called Karisoke.

For the first eighteen months, Fossey lived in a tent with a cot and a packing crate that served as a table for her typewriter. Clotheslines hung near the top of the tent for clothes that were almost always wet from the rain. Despite these conditions, though, she wrote, "It was impossible to feel lonely. The night sounds . . . encompassed me as part of the tranquillity of the nights. Those were magical times."[6]

After a year and a half, a one-room cabin replaced the tent. Later, larger cabins replaced the first one-room cabin. Additional cabins soon housed students who came to study the gorillas that Dian Fossey had habituated.

▷ In the Parc National des Volcans

In Rwanda's Parc National des Volcans, Fossey found an environment very different from the one at Kabara. Small farms crowded the edge of the park, and people went into the park to collect wood for fires and bees to make honey. Cattle grazed inside the park's boundaries, and poachers set traps to catch small antelope. Gorillas, unfortunately, were often the unintended victims of these traps.

Even though it was illegal to hunt or keep cattle in the park, the Rwandan government employed only a few guards there to enforce laws that no one seemed to take seriously. Instead of arresting people who hunted in the park, the guards took payment from them in the form of meat or milk and sometimes cash.[7]

A War Against Poachers

From her first days at Karisoke until the end of her life, Dian Fossey's work with the gorillas included an unrelenting war against anything that threatened them or their habitat. She searched for and destroyed trap lines. She herded cattle out of the park. She raided the huts used by poachers and cattle herders. She even captured a ten-year-old boy, the son of a poacher known to her, as the boy was taking aim at an antelope. She kept the boy captive for two days before returning him to his father in exchange for the father's promise to stop hunting and trapping in the gorillas' territory. She later wrote that "the hostage enjoyed his two-day stay at camp" and that the father kept his promise, at least for a while.[8]

Very early in her antipoaching efforts, Fossey listened to the arguments of a friend, a Belgian woman who had lived in Africa most of her life. As Fossey broke bamboo traps, her friend argued that the land belonged to the Africans, not to an American woman. Fossey was able to concede that people there poached just to survive when she wrote, "Maybe she is right,

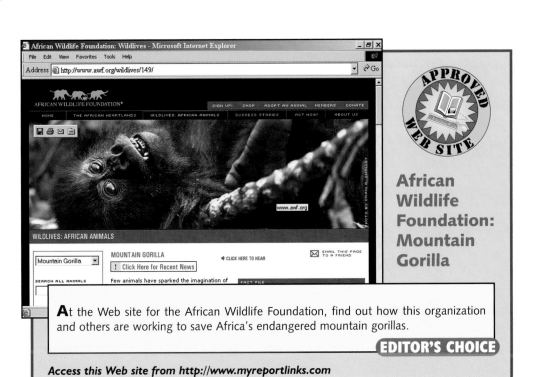

African Wildlife Foundation: Wildlives - Microsoft Internet Explorer

File Edit View Favorites Tools Help

Address http://www.awf.org/wildlives/149/

AFRICAN WILDLIFE FOUNDATION®

SIGN UP!   SHOP   ADOPT AN ANIMAL   MEMBERS   DONATE

HOME   THE AFRICAN HEARTLANDS   WILDLIVES: AFRICAN ANIMALS   SUCCESS STORIES   ACT NOW!   ABOUT US

www.awf.org

WILDLIVES: AFRICAN ANIMALS

Mountain Gorilla

MOUNTAIN GORILLA

CLICK HERE TO HEAR

EMAIL THIS PAGE TO A FRIEND

Click Here for Recent News

SEARCH ALL ANIMALS

Few animals have sparked the imagination of

FACT FILE

At the Web site for the African Wildlife Foundation, find out how this organization and others are working to save Africa's endangered mountain gorillas.

EDITOR'S CHOICE

African Wildlife Foundation: Mountain Gorilla

Access this Web site from http://www.myreportlinks.com

for the country African living on the fringes of a park area has little alternative but to turn to poaching for his livelihood." Still she continued to destroy traps, because she believed that the animals in the park were her first responsibility.[9]

▶ Friendship

As she waged war on human threats to the gorillas, Fossey became familiar with the gorillas themselves. She numbered gorilla families as she came in contact with them, and she named the individual gorillas. Whinny was the name she chose for the silverback leader of Group 4 because his roar sounded like a horse's whinny. She later learned that Whinny's raspy sound was caused by his lungs deteriorating. Digit was a five-year-old juvenile with a crooked finger. An older female became Old Goat. Fossey named a younger silverback Uncle Bert because he looked like her uncle. She wrote that she considered the name a compliment but it was one her relative never appreciated. Young females became Bravado, Maisie, Petula, and Macho (Swahili for "eyes").

Fossey was eventually accepted by the gorillas in her study area, but the acceptance took years to earn. She spent many hours sitting nearby, pretending to eat wild celery and imitating their vocalizations. She did not follow the gorillas when they left; she did not want them to see her as a pursuer.[10]

Bushmeat Project

One of the reasons that gorillas are facing extinction is the growing demand for their meat. At this Web site, learn about the bushmeat trade in Africa and its effect on gorilla populations.

Access this Web site from http://www.myreportlinks.com

First Touch

The first physical contact came two and a half years after she established Karisoke, when a gorilla she had named Peanuts touched her outstretched hand. She spent most of her time with Uncle Bert's family, Group 4, and became close to them. Young gorillas climbed on her, and adult gorillas sat with her, touching her hair or looking into her eyes.

Gorilla Observations

Dian Fossey had many opportunities to watch young gorillas at play. Once she watched the silverback Uncle Bert lead five young gorillas in his family in what she described as a "square-dance type of game. . . . Loping from one tree to the next, each animal extended its arms to grab a trunk for a quick twirl before repeating the same maneuver with the next tree down the line." She described the end of the line as "a big pile-up of bouncing bodies and broken branches." Again and again, Uncle Bert led his group up the slope for "another go-around with the splintered tree remnants."[11]

Another time she watched as a two-and-a-half-year-old named Tiger tried to build his own day nest. Fossey noted that Tiger began by bending long stalks of leaves onto his lap as he had seen adults do. But when he tried to sit on his nest, the stalks sprang up; he just did not weigh enough to hold them down. After several attempts, Tiger grew frustrated and swatted at

It took time and patience for Dian Fossey to earn the trust of the mountain gorillas of the Virunga chain. These mountain gorillas were most likely easier to approach and photograph than they would have been when Fossey first began her research.

the foliage, "before jumping up and twirling rapidly in a circle to plop on his back, spreadeagled, in a last futile effort to hold down the unruly stalks," according to Fossey. Finally Tiger went to rest with his mother in her nest.[12]

Fossey also watched the natural transition from one silverback leader to another. As Whinny became weaker and weaker from pneumonia, the group traveled more slowly. When the old silverback died, one of his sons, Uncle Bert, was ready to lead the family, and the family was able to stay together.

Active Conservation

Over the years, Dian Fossey became more frustrated with the handful of park guards paid by the Rwandan government to protect the park. When she arrived in 1967, there were only about a dozen guards to patrol the 50,000-acre (20,235-hectare) park. She soon concluded that the guards were afraid to venture into the forest.[13] People living on the edge of starvation did not care about the gorillas or the gorillas' habitat, but Fossey believed it was her job to protect the animals.

Although Dian Fossey made an effort to work with the Rwandan government, she felt she could be of greater service to the gorillas by hiring, outfitting, and training her own antipoacher teams. In her mind, "active conservation" meant driving poachers away from the gorillas. Antipoacher patrols made up of Rwandan employees and research students set out from Karisoke to comb the forest for traps. They cut traps, freed newly trapped animals, and took whatever they found that belonged to poachers.

International Fame

Between chasing poachers, destroying wire traps, harassing trespassing cattle, and observing gorillas, Fossey found time to write articles for *National Geographic* magazine. A photographer filmed footage of Fossey for a *National Geographic* documentary. Through the *National Geographic* articles and television documentaries, as well as her own public-speaking tours, the Western world came to know the gorillas of Fossey's study groups. The presidents of Rwanda and Zaire asked Fossey to give her gorilla presentation for them.[14]

With her years of research into gorilla behavior, Fossey was accepted as a Ph.D. candidate at England's Cambridge University. In 1974, she received her doctorate in zoology. The therapist who had first traveled to Africa eleven years earlier because of her fascination with the continent and its animals was now Dr. Fossey, the world's foremost expert on mountain gorillas.

Digit

As gorillas became better known in Europe and the United States, Rwandan tourism officials thought the gorillas might attract tourists to the Parc des Volcans and boost the country's economy. Although Fossey did not like the idea of tourists bothering her gorillas, she

Gorillas: Animal Information, Pictures, Map--National Geographic Kids - Microsoft Internet Explorer

File Edit View Favorites Tools Help

Address http://www.nationalgeographic.com/kids/creature_feature/0007/gorillas.html Go

NATIONALGEOGRAPHIC.COM Kids   Parents NationalGeographic.com Home

Kids Home   NG Kids Magazine   NG Explorer Classroom Magazine   Games   Activities Experiments   Homework Help   Kids News

Creature Feature   Fun Facts

MOUNTAIN GORILLAS

Video
RealPlayer
Windows Media
Help

Audio

Map

Postcard

Photograph above by Stuart Perimeter
Photograph at top left by Dian Fossey
credits

NATIONALGEOGRAPHIC.COM Kids   Kids Home   NG Kids Magazine   NG Explorer Classroom Magazine

Creature Feature: Mountain Gorillas

This *National Geographic* site takes a look at the life and times of Rwanda's mountain gorillas. *National Geographic* photographs and a television special in the 1970s helped focus the world's attention on Dian Fossey and her gorillas.

Access this Web site from http://www.myreportlinks.com

supplied a photograph to be used in a poster that beckoned "Come to meet him in Rwanda." The gorilla in the photograph was Digit.

Fossey's first contact with Digit had been when he was a fluffy, curious five-year-old. She watched him grow into a mature and responsible silverback leader. Digit supported Uncle Bert in conflicts that arose when his family encountered another family, and he took sentry duty at the edge of the group.

Then on December 31, 1977, Digit, acting as sentry, stood his ground in front of poachers as his family fled. The poachers' spears killed Digit, and the poachers hacked off his head and hands. On February 3, 1978, an American news broadcast led with a report of

Digit's death. Millions of Americans had seen Digit not long before in a *National Geographic* television program and felt they knew him.

More Deaths

About seven months later, poachers shot Uncle Bert as he protected his family. Apparently the poachers intended to kidnap a three-year-old gorilla named Kweli and sell him to a zoo. Kweli's mother, Macho, was also shot. Kweli escaped but with a bullet wound in his shoulder. Three months later he, too, died. With no younger silverback to take Uncle Bert's place and keep the family together, the four females soon transferred to other gorilla groups, and more deaths resulted.

The silverback gorillas that are so gentle with the infants in their own families will not tolerate the infant offspring of other silverbacks. When females with infants transfer to other families, the silverbacks dispose of the tiny infants with a quick bite or a blow to the head. Two of the Group 4 females carried infants that died as a result of this practice of infanticide. The attempt to capture little Kweli, probably for sale to a zoo, resulted in five gorilla deaths.

The Digit Fund

The gorilla deaths fueled Fossey's determination to provide "active conservation," her term for antipoaching efforts. She established the Digit Fund (now the Dian Fossey Gorilla Fund International) to raise money so that Rwandans could be hired and trained to carry out antipoaching patrols. Her fund-raising efforts did not produce as much money as she had hoped. Still, in 1983, Fossey reported that antipoaching patrols paid for by the Digit Fund had destroyed 1,701 traps set by poachers.[15]

One More Death

During the early 1980s, Fossey spent most of her time in the United States. She taught at Cornell University in Ithaca, New York, and in 1983 published *Gorillas in the Mist,* about her life and work in Africa with mountain gorillas, which was later adapted and made into a

projects page - Microsoft Internet Explorer

File   Edit   View   Favorites   Tools   Help

Address http://www.dianfossey.org/portfolio.html   Go

picture portfolio
as close as you — can get without — actually being there

Unaware of her own destiny, Dian examines Carl Akeleys grave at the edge of the Kabara meadow

Dian watches Rafiki and Pe exposed on a fallen Hageni

More photos of Dian Fossey, Rwanda, and the mountain gorillas she loved can be found on **The Dian Fossey Gorilla Fund** Web site.

film. When Fossey returned to Karisoke after being away for three years, her reunion with the gorillas was, as she wrote, one of the outstanding moments of her life. Four older female gorillas came to her, stared her in the eyes, and embraced her.[16]

The researcher did not have much longer to spend with the animals she so loved, however. In December 1985, Dian Fossey was found murdered in her cabin at Karisoke. A Rwandan suspect died in jail, and an American research student who had worked with Fossey was tried in absentia and found guilty but remains free. (The United States has no extradition agreement with Rwanda, so the American cannot be forced to travel there and stand trial.) Many people who knew Fossey believe that her murderer, most likely a poacher she angered, has yet to be found.

Dian Fossey was buried in a small cemetery at Karisoke next to the grave of her beloved Digit. A marker on her grave reads simply but profoundly, "No one loved gorillas more."

Chapter 5

NEW DIRECTIONS FOR GORILLA CONSERVATION

Many people in the United States and in the United Kingdom felt Digit's death as a personal loss because they had seen him in *National Geographic* articles and in television documentaries. News of the gorilla's death brought increased donations to conservation organizations, especially the Fauna and Flora Preservation Society in England and the African Wildlife Leadership Foundation in the United States. These funds made it possible to consider new efforts to save the mountain gorillas.

▶ The Mountain Gorilla Project

For some time, Rwanda's department of tourism, the Office Rwandais du Tourisme et de Parc Nationaux (ORTPN), had hoped to bring money to Rwanda by encouraging tourists to come see the gorillas. However, in 1978, the park earned less than $7,000 in entry fees.[1] By 1979, the Rwandan government had developed a plan to make the park more profitable. The plan involved clearing 12,500 acres (5,059 hectares) of parkland, about one third of the remaining land, for a cattle-raising project. Rwandan officials

Welcome to Fauna & Flora International

Fauna & Flora International (FFI) is the world's longest
established international conservation body, founded over 100
years ago. Renowned for its science-based approach, FFI has
pioneered sustainable conservation work that tackles
problems holistically, providing solutions that simultaneously
help wildlife, humans and the environment.

FFI acts to conserve threatened species and ecosystems
worldwide, choosing solutions that are sustainable, are based
on sound science and take account of human needs.

Environmental Management Through Precaution

The Precautionary Principle Project is a joint initiative of FFI,
ResourceAfrica, IUCN and TRAFFIC and seeks to develop
"best practice" guidance on the meaning and application of
precaution in natural resource management and biodiversity
conservation. Guidelines for applying the precautionary
principle are now available following an extensive process of
research and consultation. Available in English, French and
Spanish the guidelines can be downloaded from the

Fauna and Flora International, founded more than one hundred years ago, is a
partner with other conservation groups in helping to save mountain gorillas. Learn
more about this group's work from its Web site.

Access this Web site from http://www.myreportlinks.com

anticipated profits of $70,000 per year.[2] That amount
of money would be very useful in a poor country, but
conservationists believed the land was needed for
gorilla habitat if gorillas were to survive. To save the
parkland for the gorillas, conservationists would need
to come up with another plan to raise money without
harming the gorillas.

A partnership quickly formed between ORTPN, Fauna
and Flora International (then known as the Fauna
and Flora Preservation Society), the African Wildlife
Foundation (then the African Wildlife Leadership
Foundation), and the World Wildlife Fund to put in
place a plan to save the gorillas.[3] The goals of the plan
were to end poaching in the park, educate Rwandans

about the value of the gorillas and the Virunga rain forest, and bring tourists to spend time with gorillas and spend dollars in Rwanda. The plan became known as the Mountain Gorilla Project (MGP). Leaders of the project included two former students at Karisoke, Alexander (Sandy) Harcourt and Bill Weber.

Gorilla Tourism

Tourism was an essential part of the Mountain Gorilla Project's plan. A successful program would bring money to Rwanda and create jobs around the park. Program developers hoped money and increased employment could quickly change public opinion about the park's value.

This Australian news article examines twin births in mountain gorillas, a rarity in the species as far as researchers know.

Access this Web site from http://www.myreportlinks.com

At the same time, increased tourism did not come without risk. Because the gorillas are shy, continued exposure to unfamiliar people would be stressful to them. Conservationists wondered if the stress might be enough to weaken the gorillas' immune systems at the same time that the animals would be exposed to human diseases. Tourism might also cause the gorillas to look for new territories or reduce female transfers to new families.[4] Finally, there was no such thing as ecotourism in 1979. Would people really be willing to climb the steep mountainsides, hiking through mud the entire way, just to see gorillas?

Since tourism offered the possibility of making the park and the gorillas valuable to the Rwandans, Bill Weber set about using his Karisoke experience to habituate gorilla families so that tourists would be able to visit them. The research gorillas would be left to the researchers.

▶ Habituation

The habituation process began with daily visits to the gorilla family by Weber and a Rwandan named Nemeye. The two would approach the gorilla group and then kneel and pretend to eat as they used the belch vocalizations that Dian Fossey had taught all Karisoke researchers. At first the gorillas simply left, retreating into the dense foliage. Then Stilgar, the silverback leader of one family, began to scream and charged the two men, insisting on privacy. Another lesson Weber had learned from Dian Fossey was to hold his ground in the face of the 350-pound gorilla's charge. After a few days, Stilgar's charges stopped. Instead, he chose to sit and stare at the visitors while his family stayed hidden. Finally, after several weeks, the curiosity of the young gorillas prevailed, and they were allowed to stay in full view, watching the visitors.

Eventually, Weber brought "practice" tourists to visit Stilgar and his family. Stilgar was not pleased, but

△ *Though gorilla tourism is helping to save mountain gorillas, precautions need to be taken to protect the tourists from the animals—and the animals from the tourists.*

the young gorillas seemed to enjoy them, according to Weber: "Each of the juveniles approached the visitors differently: some sneaked up behind us, others ambled slowly past. One preferred aerial reconnaissance from overhanging branches and bamboo."[5] But the young gorillas' interest presented a new challenge. To protect both the gorillas and the tourists, they would have to be kept apart. The guides kept a close eye on tourists and used cough grunts, the sounds gorilla parents make when disciplining their young, to keep the young gorillas at a safe distance.

▶ Stilgar in Charge

Stilgar became habituated, but he was still in charge of his family. And he was not about to let anyone forget that fact. One morning, Weber and Nemeye took two women to visit the gorillas. They found the gorillas munching leaves in a shallow crater. Soon the visitors were leaning over a fallen tree, watching the gorillas below them. Suddenly, as Weber wrote later, "two immense black hands rose up and slapped the trunk right in front of them."[6] Stilgar's enormous head rose above the trunk, just a few feet from the visitors, and the gorilla stared at his visitors. Then he went back down the hill as quietly as he had come up it.

The tourist program established rules to protect the gorillas. One rule was that groups visiting the gorillas should include no more than six people. Small groups were considered less stressful for the gorillas, who

TRAFFIC

Access this Web site from http://www.myreportlinks.com

TRAFFIC, in cooperation with the IUCN and CITES, monitors the illegal international trade of wildlife. Information on poaching, the illegal selling of animal parts, and conservation measures are available on this site.

EDITOR'S CHOICE

were more comfortable when they could see all of their visitors. It was also easier to control a small group to prevent any physical contact between tourists and curious young gorillas.

Another rule was that visits should last no more than an hour and should be timed to match the gorillas' mid-morning rest period. Interestingly, Stilgar apparently approved of this rule. Whenever tourists arrived, whether it was at nine or eleven in the morning, he and the adult females would find an area where they could watch the visitors and take a break. After about an hour, the gorilla family would get up and leave to resume eating.[7]

Success

The tourist program quickly showed its potential as an important source of revenue for Rwanda. More than one thousand tourists paid to see the gorillas during the program's first year. Hotels, restaurants, and car-rental agencies began to see increased business, and more guards were hired to patrol the Parc National des Volcans. The number of guards went from fourteen to more than forty. Even more important, the guards received training and equipment, such as boots and rain gear, that had been lacking for some time.[8]

The tourism program continued to grow, and within a decade, the park was earning almost $1 million per year. Only coffee and tea exports brought more foreign dollars to Rwanda.[9]

▷ Educating Local People

An important part of the Mountain Gorilla Project was education. The project partnership believed that it was important that Rwandans learn about the gorillas in their country so that they would want to protect them.

At the time, there were more than 100,000 farmers living within five miles of the Parc National des Volcans.[10] Surveys of the local farmers revealed that, generally, they had nothing against the gorillas. When they learned that there were only 260 gorillas left, the farmers agreed that the animals should be protected. But the farmers also believed that they should be able to hunt

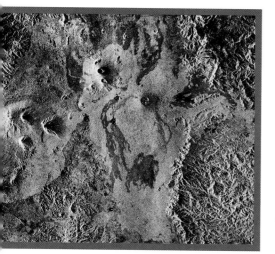

◁ This NASA satellite image shows the Virunga volcanic range, home to the mountain gorillas.

and collect wood in the park. They also wanted to farm the park's forested land, although none of their crops would grow at such high altitudes. For people desperate for land to grow food for their families, the park as a forested refuge had no value.

The farmers did not understand the importance of the park's forest in terms of their own farmland. The forests covering the steep slopes of the Virunga volcanoes helped to prevent flooding of the surrounding areas. Perhaps more important, the forest captured water and filtered it through the soil. The clear mountain water flowed steadily in streams to the farmland below. Clearing the remaining forest would mean alternating floods and drought in the farmers' fields and severe soil erosion.

The Mountain Gorilla Project produced a film about the importance of people and gorillas coexisting and presented it to secondary schools around Rwanda. The MGP also took its presentation to primary schools close to the park, since many of those children would never go to secondary school but would continue to live close to the gorillas. The film was also shown to adults living in communities bordering the park.

Antipoaching Successes

An important part of the Mountain Gorilla Project that was successful was its drive to prevent poaching in the Parc National des Volcans. The additional park guards who were trained and equipped as professionals took

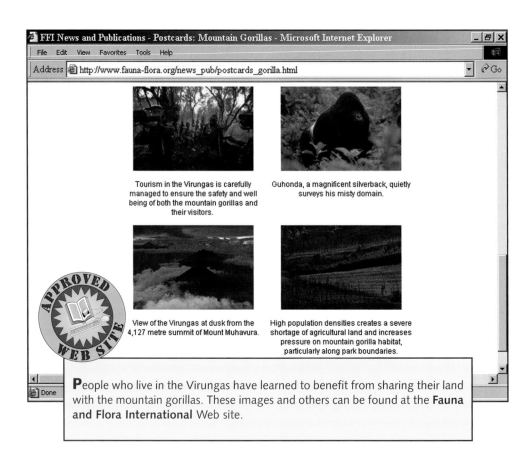

FFI News and Publications - Postcards: Mountain Gorillas - Microsoft Internet Explorer

File   Edit   View   Favorites   Tools   Help

Address   http://www.fauna-flora.org/news_pub/postcards_gorilla.html

Tourism in the Virungas is carefully managed to ensure the safety and well being of both the mountain gorillas and their visitors.

Guhonda, a magnificent silverback, quietly surveys his misty domain.

View of the Virungas at dusk from the 4,127 metre summit of Mount Muhavura.

High population densities creates a severe shortage of agricultural land and increases pressure on mountain gorilla habitat, particularly along park boundaries.

People who live in the Virungas have learned to benefit from sharing their land with the mountain gorillas. These images and others can be found at the **Fauna and Flora International** Web site.

their work seriously. But other aspects of the Mountain Gorilla Project also reduced poaching in the park.

As guides took tourists to see the gorillas on an almost daily basis, they watched for snares and evidence of poachers. Conservationists noticed that more infants were born in groups habituated for research and for tourism. Because of the increased protection, the population of the mountain gorillas was increasing for the first time since the gorillas began losing habitat in the 1950s.[11] And as local people benefited from tourism, the park and its contents began to have value in their eyes. The Rwandan guides who led the tourists through the forest became important people in the community.

The Other Gorillas

While the gorillas of the Virunga volcanoes were gaining the world's attention, the mountain gorillas of Uganda's Bwindi Impenetrable National Park quietly faced similar challenges. This park is also surrounded by farmers who can barely grow enough food for their families to live on. Poachers trap animals in the park, and people enter the forest to cut wood, collect honey, and search for gold, which has been found there. During times of political upheavals, in the 1970s and early 1980s, Uganda's Forest Department failed to enforce laws that protected the land, which was then a forest reserve, and the animals that lived on it.[12]

The forest reserve became a national park in 1991. The Mountain Gorilla Project evolved into the International Gorilla Conservation Programme, and with its help, Uganda began a gorilla tourism program in 1993. The park soon began earning about $1 million per year.[13]

In 1996, scientists began a study of the mountain gorillas in the Bwindi Impenetrable National Park. One gorilla family has been habituated, and researchers have accumulated information about what the gorillas eat, how far they travel in a day, and where they build

http://www.mountaingorillas.org/images/Mubare_Jan_2002.jpg - Microsoft Internet Explorer

This page from the Web site of the **International Gorilla Conservation Programme** presents a mountain gorilla family group living in the Bwindi Impenetrable National Park in Uganda.

EDITOR'S CHOICE

their nests. One interesting finding is that the Bwindi gorillas eat fruit during certain seasons, probably because it is available. Bwindi gorillas are also more likely to build their night nests in trees. The park is also an area where gorillas and chimpanzees live together. Researchers are eager to learn how the two related species interact.

GORILLA SURVIVAL IN THE MIDST OF TURMOIL

In 1989, conservationists trekked through the Virunga volcanoes to count the Virunga mountain gorillas—and celebrated cautiously. The census takers were able to find evidence of about three hundred gorillas in the area. This increase since the 1978 count, which had found 260 gorillas, was especially encouraging in a species in which females usually give birth only once every four years.

▶ Trouble in Rwanda

While the 1980s were good years for the gorillas of Rwanda, they were not as kind to the people of that country. In Rwanda, coffee had become one of the country's leading exports. When a worldwide overabundance of coffee sent prices spiraling downward, Rwanda's economy was devastated. Toward the end of the decade, a drought killed the crops of subsistence farmers. To make matters worse, corruption in the government led many Rwandans to mistrust their leaders.[1]

Perhaps because of all these things, Rwandans' distrust of each other grew as well. In 1990, organized Tutsi refugees of the Rwandan Patriotic Front (RPF) fought their way into northern Rwanda to rebel against the Hutu government. The RPF was defeated and, as the fighters fled, they hid in the Virunga volcanoes. In the wake of the RPF defeat, many Rwandan Tutsis were killed. Demonstrations became more violent, political leaders were assassinated, and a radio station broadcast messages of hate. A group of extremist Hutus known as *Interahamwe,* or "those who work together," began to murder Tutsis and moderate Hutus.

▶ Genocide and War

Toward the end of 1993, the United Nations sent peacekeepers to the region. The commander of the U.N. forces, concerned about the level of violence and

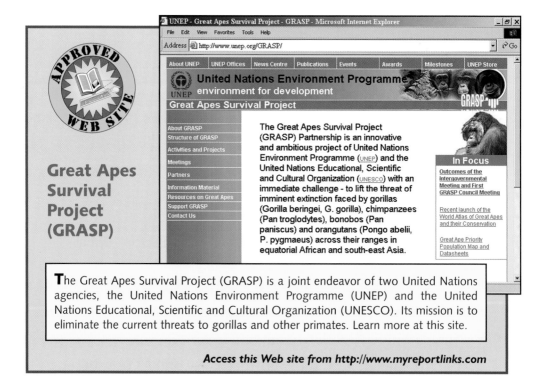

Great Apes Survival Project (GRASP)

UNEP - Great Apes Survival Project - GRASP - Microsoft Internet Explorer

File Edit View Favorites Tools Help

Address http://www.unep.org/GRASP/

About UNEP | UNEP Offices | News Centre | Publications | Events | Awards | Milestones | UNEP Store

United Nations Environment Programme
UNEP environment for development
Great Apes Survival Project

About GRASP
Structure of GRASP
Activities and Projects
Meetings
Partners
Information Material
Resources on Great Apes
Support GRASP
Contact Us

The Great Apes Survival Project (GRASP) Partnership is an innovative and ambitious project of United Nations Environment Programme (UNEP) and the United Nations Educational, Scientific and Cultural Organization (UNESCO) with an immediate challenge - to lift the threat of imminent extinction faced by gorillas (Gorilla beringei, G. gorilla), chimpanzees (Pan troglodytes), bonobos (Pan paniscus) and orangutans (Pongo abelii, P. pygmaeus) across their ranges in equatorial African and south-east Asia.

In Focus

Outcomes of the Intergovernmental Meeting and First GRASP Council Meeting

Recent launch of the World Atlas of Great Apes and their Conservation

Great Ape Priority Population Map and Datasheets

The Great Apes Survival Project (GRASP) is a joint endeavor of two United Nations agencies, the United Nations Environment Programme (UNEP) and the United Nations Educational, Scientific and Cultural Organization (UNESCO). Its mission is to eliminate the current threats to gorillas and other primates. Learn more at this site.

Access this Web site from http://www.myreportlinks.com

hate, asked for more troops to stop the killing, but his request was denied.

In April 1994, genocide ripped the country apart, as an estimated 800,000 Tutsis and moderate Hutus were killed by their own countrymen. When the RPF retaliated and overthrew the Hutu government, about 2 million Hutu refugees fled to neighboring countries.[2]

Violence soon flared all around the gorillas. As the RPF pursued Hutu leaders into the neighboring Congo, many Congolese encouraged them to overthrow Mobutu Sese Seko, the president of their own country who ruled as a dictator. Soon both Rwanda and Uganda had soldiers in the Congo, and in 1997, Mobutu was overthrown. Laurent Kabila, the Congo's new leader, asked for help from the neighboring countries of Zimbabwe, Angola, and Sudan.[3] The war begun in Rwanda had spread, resulting in the deaths of more than a million people.

Most Rwandan refugees were forced to return to their country in 1996, but reconciliation has been difficult among people whose memories of the horrors of genocide are still fresh. The first presidential and legislative election after the killings did not take place until 2003.

Gorillas and Refugees

On a single day in July 1994, about 500,000 Rwandan refugees arrived at refugee camps set up on the edge of the Virunga National Park, on the Congo side of the gorillas' habitat. Within just a few days, more than 300,000 followed.[4] Many of the refugees fled through the Virunga parklands to cross the border into the Congo, causing damage throughout the forest where the gorillas lived.

Once in the refugee camps, people desperately looked for ways to survive. They turned to the parkland for wood to use for building and for fuel. Tree cutting affected more than 40 square miles (100 square kilometers) of the Virunga National Park in the DRC.[5] Some areas were completely cleared.

People also entered the forested parkland to hunt for food. Poachers' snares were not the only problem for wildlife. Guerrilla fighters with guns entered the Virunga rain forest from all directions to stage attacks in Rwanda and the Congo. Between 1995 and 1998, sixteen mountain gorillas were killed in the Congo side of the Virunga volcanoes.[6]

▶ Gorilla Conservation Continues

War did not stop the efforts to save the gorillas, but priorities changed. The first priority was paying the salaries of park guards and providing equipment. Amazingly, many park guards continued to patrol the parklands in spite of the great danger—and in spite of the government upheavals that made their employment uncertain. Some rangers were ambushed and killed. In 1996, the J. Paul Getty Wildlife Conservation Prize, awarded for outstanding efforts in international conservation, was given to the Parc National des Volcans. It recognized the park staff's heroic acts in protecting the refuge's mountain gorillas during the Rwandan civil war.[7]

Even after the war ended, however, the Virunga rain forest was a dangerous place. Land mines left behind killed two gorillas and made any future tourism very risky. The task of clearing the forest of the land mines was shared by members of the new

▲ If mountain gorillas are to survive, it is crucial that the people of Rwanda—and those of the Congo and Uganda—learn to value these gentle primates that share their homelands. Here, at the entrance of the Parc National des Volcans, Rwandan officials speak to local schoolchildren about the importance of conservation and the threat of poaching.

▲ A young mountain gorilla emerges from the dense foliage of the rain forest.

Rwandan army. Five soldiers spent two years crawling through the forest, moving machetes just above the ground to find the mines.[8]

Those who carried on the work of Dian Fossey at Karisoke also struggled through great difficulties during the 1990s. Karisoke's staff members were robbed, and equipment was stolen from their homes. The trackers turned to the Rwandan army for help and were given military escorts. Trackers were also given paramilitary training by the army.[9]

The center itself, established by Fossey in 1967, was destroyed in 1994. But its programs are still carried out by the Dian Fossey Gorilla Fund International in a house in the town of Ruhengeri, which is a short distance by car from the Parc National des Volcans.

A Delicate Balance

While armed park guards did what they could to protect the mountain gorillas, conservationists did what they could to protect the gorillas' habitat. Planting trees on deforested land was one priority. When they learned that the Rwandan government planned to resettle refugees within the park boundaries, conservationists convinced government officials to abandon that plan. Conservationists also got the government to give up its plans to build a road through the park. Both conservationists and government officials have come to realize that tourism, the welfare of local people, and the fate of the gorillas are linked in a delicate balance.[10]

HOPE FOR THE FUTURE

In 1960, zoologist George Schaller estimated that there were about 450 gorillas in the Virunga mountains. A more precise census was conducted between 1971 and 1973, and the final count was disturbing. Conservationists found evidence of only 275 gorillas.

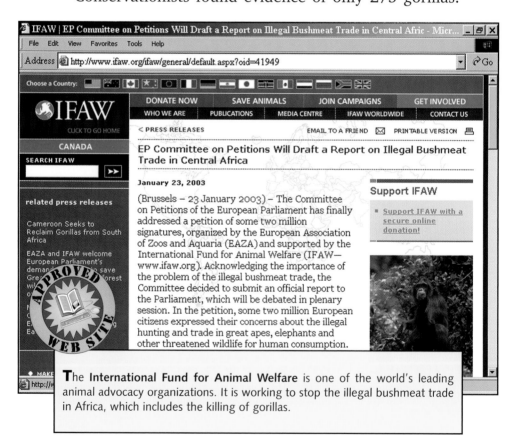

IFAW | EP Committee on Petitions Will Draft a Report on Illegal Bushmeat Trade in Central Afric - Micr...

File   Edit   View   Favorites   Tools   Help

Address http://www.ifaw.org/ifaw/general/default.aspx?oid=41949   Go

Choose a Country:

IFAW
CLICK TO GO HOME

DONATE NOW   SAVE ANIMALS   JOIN CAMPAIGNS   GET INVOLVED
WHO WE ARE   PUBLICATIONS   MEDIA CENTRE   IFAW WORLDWIDE   CONTACT US

CANADA

SEARCH IFAW

< PRESS RELEASES   EMAIL TO A FRIEND   PRINTABLE VERSION

EP Committee on Petitions Will Draft a Report on Illegal Bushmeat Trade in Central Africa

January 23, 2003

related press releases

Cameroon Seeks to Reclaim Gorillas from South Africa

EAZA and IFAW welcome European Parliament's demand to save Great ... forest wil...

(Brussels – 23 January 2003) – The Committee on Petitions of the European Parliament has finally addressed a petition of some two million signatures, organized by the European Association of Zoos and Aquaria (EAZA) and supported by the International Fund for Animal Welfare (IFAW– www.ifaw.org). Acknowledging the importance of the problem of the illegal bushmeat trade, the Committee decided to submit an official report to the Parliament, which will be debated in plenary session. In the petition, some two million European citizens expressed their concerns about the illegal hunting and trade in great apes, elephants and other threatened wildlife for human consumption.

Support IFAW

▪ Support IFAW with a secure online donation!

APPROVED WEB SITE

The International Fund for Animal Welfare is one of the world's leading animal advocacy organizations. It is working to stop the illegal bushmeat trade in Africa, which includes the killing of gorillas.

Another census taken later in the 1970s counted 268 gorillas. By 1981, when a third census was taken, the news was worse. Researchers counted only 254 gorillas.[1]

During the 1970s, many experts were convinced that the mountain gorilla would become extinct in the same century in which it was discovered. The good news today is that mountain gorillas are not extinct. In fact, gorillas survived a very turbulent time in the region and even increased in number. A regional census done in 2003 found 380 gorillas.[2] Another three hundred mountain gorillas live in the Bwindi Impenetrable National Park, bringing the total to about seven hundred. The population increase is an encouraging sign.

▶ Conservation in the Twenty-first Century

Also encouraging is the continued work being done by conservationists to save mountain gorillas. Dian Fossey's work is continued by members of the Dian Fossey Gorilla Fund International, even though the original Karisoke station was destroyed. The new center, at Ruhengeri, employs almost 40 trackers and antipoachers and provides a base for researchers and scientists.[3]

The new Karisoke continues to study the gorillas in three families and protect gorillas throughout the park. Research includes studies of gorilla temperament, gorilla ranging patterns, the impact of tourism on the gorillas, and other aspects of gorilla life. Protection has been expanded to gorillas far from the research area.

Karisoke antipoaching teams and park guards set up campsites deep in the forest to patrol the surrounding area for a week at a time.[4]

Today, while trackers continue to walk through the forest to monitor gorillas, they have new tools. Global Positioning System (GPS) technology enables trackers to record data with greater accuracy. Computers allow GPS information to be combined with "remote sensing" information collected by satellite technology to offer broad views of changes in the gorilla habitat and in areas surrounding the gorillas. The new information-gathering tools are a result of partnerships between conservation groups, universities, scientists, and local governments.

▶ Tourism

Tourism continues to aid conservation, bringing money to impoverished, war-torn countries and keeping people around the world in touch with the gorillas. War interrupted tourism several times during the 1990s, but governments in the gorillas' three host countries hope to prevent future interruptions. In spite of continued unrest and occasional fighting on the ground, the DRC, Rwanda, and Uganda signed an agreement in 2001 in which they agreed to work together to protect the gorillas and their habitat.[5] And in working together to save the region's gorillas, the countries involved are also working toward peace in their part of Africa.

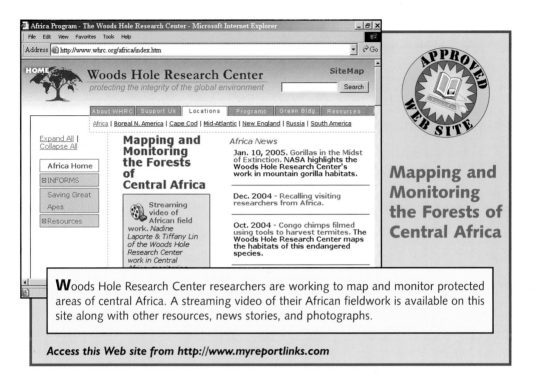

Woods Hole Research Center researchers are working to map and monitor protected areas of central Africa. A streaming video of their African fieldwork is available on this site along with other resources, news stories, and photographs.

Access this Web site from http://www.myreportlinks.com

▶ Expanded View of Conservation

While the conservation efforts begun in the twentieth century continue, conservation in the twenty-first century includes a greater emphasis on partnerships, especially with the people who live close to the gorillas. The Dian Fossey Gorilla Fund International, through the Karisoke Research Center, partners with the National University of Rwanda in providing scientific supervision and financial support for students studying biodiversity and conservation. Karisoke staff also provide training for park guards employed by ORTPN in Rwanda.[6]

Another example of the partnerships formed to help both the gorillas and their human neighbors is a ranger-based monitoring program begun in the Congo by the International Gorilla Conservation Programme in 1996. Most of the rangers are local people without scientific training who patrol the parks to collect information. Sometimes, rangers may carry only paper and pencil, but they often use GPS technology as well. The rangers pass on information to park authorities who use it to make decisions about where the gorillas are feeding and where antipoaching patrols should be sent. Ranger-based monitoring now extends throughout the gorillas' habitat in all three countries.[7]

▶ More Partnerships

A partnership that was begun in 1986 continues to provide veterinary care for the mountain gorillas. When DFGFI asked the Morris Animal Foundation to help care for the gorillas, the foundation provided a clinic to care for gorillas suffering from human-caused illnesses and injuries.

In the 1990s, the project became the Mountain Gorilla Veterinary Project (MGVP), and its efforts expanded to include information gathering and storing. The MGVP also developed a program to monitor the health of people working with mountain gorillas so that those people would not pass on human diseases to the animals.[8]

No mountain gorilla has ever survived in captivity, so conservation measures must focus on preserving their habitat. Learn more about what is being done to preserve the home of mountain gorillas when you visit this organization's Web site.

EDITOR'S CHOICE

Access this Web site from http://www.myreportlinks.com

A Partners in Conservation program began in 1991 when staff and volunteers at the Columbus Zoo in Columbus, Ohio, learned about the war in Rwanda and its effect on the mountain gorillas in the region. The founders of this partnership realized that the fate of the gorillas is intertwined with the fate of their neighbors. The program's goals are to educate Americans about the gorillas and about the people of the Congo, Rwanda, and Uganda and to raise money for those people and the wildlife. One method of raising money is through the sale of handcrafted items from the Congo and Rwanda. People from other zoos across the United States now volunteer their time to be partners in this program.[9]

Reports From the Field

The Mountain Gorilla Veterinary Project, begun in 1986, is funded by the Morris Animal Foundation. This group of veterinarians is working to save mountain gorillas living in Rwanda and Uganda. Learn more about the project from this site.

Access this Web site from http://www.myreportlinks.com

Other partnerships came about to address specific situations. For example, the International Gorilla Conservation Programme convinced Rwandan beekeepers to move their hives outside the national park. In exchange, IGCP brought in experts to teach the Rwandans new beekeeping techniques. The training included more than just better ways to collect honey. The Rwandans also learned about marketing their honey and increasing what they earn by using the honeycomb wax to make candles.[10]

▶ Continuing Threats

Even as conservation efforts expand, the threats to the mountain gorillas of east-central Africa remain.

It is up to us to make sure that mountain gorillas like this one continue to survive.

Human pressures on all sides of the gorillas' mountain retreat are as real as ever. Poverty causes farmers to look enviously at the forest's resources. Fighting sends refugees, as well as armed soldiers, into the national parks, increasing strain on the forest environment and increasing chances that a surprised silverback will charge someone who is holding a gun. The closeness of humans also increases the likelihood that gorillas will come in contact with diseases for which they have no immunity.

In spite of increased monitoring of gorillas, poaching is still a threat. John Makombo, the man in charge of rangers in Uganda's Bwindi Impenetrable National Park, has been shot at by poachers, and he knows that poaching will continue. Poachers can sell a baby gorilla on the black market for as much as $1,000.[11] Capturing a single gorilla infant can mean killing the rest of its family.

▶ Ubuzima's Story

In 2002, poachers killed two females of a gorilla family in Rwanda. Both females, named Impanga and Muraha, had infants. When park guards discovered the gorillas' bodies, one infant was missing, but the other infant, a thirteen-month-old named Ubuzima, had spent two days close to the body of its dead mother.

Ubuzima's story illustrates the tragic results of efforts to sell baby gorillas on the black market. It also shows, however, the positive results of gorilla research and conservation partnerships. Park staff, together with conservationists from around the world and a Rwandan veterinarian from the Mountain Gorilla Veterinary Centre, quickly formed teams. One team went in search of the missing infant. Another team located the gorilla family, which was obviously frightened and did not want to be near humans. The third team, including the veterinarian, treated Ubuzima for dehydration. Once the family was located, the team with Ubuzima carried her to her family, monitoring her breathing and heart rate the entire time.

When the team members released the infant, the dominant silverback came to her and inspected her as the rest of the group watched. An older brother then took on the role of caregiver. Park guards and conservationists monitored the infant's progress. Several times, observers saw the older brother carrying Ubuzima, and the young gorilla was observed eating vegetation. At night she stayed warm as she slept between her brother and the dominant silverback. Within a month, two people were arrested in connection with the killing of the two females.[12]

Hope

The history of mountain gorilla conservation is one of commitment and sacrifice, money and creativity. Because certain people, especially Dian Fossey, cared so much about these animals, people around the world learned to care about them too. On the ground in war-ravaged countries, park rangers gave their lives defending the parks, proving the commitment of local people. Conservationists raised funds to support research and education. And creative people in many countries pushed gorilla conservation in exciting new directions.

As long as people around the world continue to care about the mountain gorillas of the Virunga volcanoes and the Bwindi Impenetrable Forest—and about the people who live close to them—mountain gorillas have a chance to survive.

In 1973, Congress took the farsighted step of creating the Endangered Species Act, widely regarded as the world's strongest and most effective wildlife conservation law. It set an ambitious goal: to reverse the alarming trend of human-caused extinction that threatened the ecosystems we all share.

Each book in this series explores the life of an endangered animal. The books tell how and why the animals have become endangered and explain the efforts being made to restore their populations.

The United States Fish and Wildlife Service and the National Marine Fisheries Service share responsibility for administration of the Endangered Species Act. Over time, animals are added to, reclassified in, or removed from the federal list of Endangered and Threatened Wildlife and Plants. At the time of publication, all the animals in this series were listed as endangered species. The most up-to-date list can be found at **http://www.fws.gov/endangered/wildlife.html**.

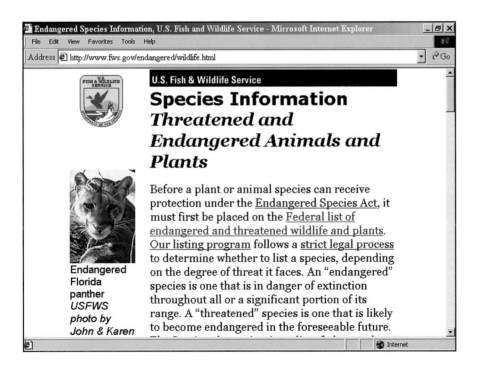

Report Links

The Internet sites described below can be accessed at http://www.myreportlinks.com

▶**Exploring the Environment: Mountain Gorillas**
Editor's Choice The mountain gorillas' struggle to survive is explained in this Web site.

▶**The Dian Fossey Gorilla Fund International**
Editor's Choice The DFGFI carries on the work of Dian Fossey to save mountain gorillas.

▶*Gorilla gorilla beringei*
Editor's Choice Information on mountain gorillas and other animals can be found on this site.

▶**African Wildlife Foundation: Mountain Gorilla**
Editor's Choice Learn how the African Wildlife Foundation has worked to save mountain gorillas.

▶**International Gorilla Conservation Programme**
Editor's Choice Information on mountain gorilla conservation is available on this site.

▶**Wildlife Conservation Society**
Editor's Choice The Wildlife Conservation Society fights to protect the wildlife of the world.

▶**Albertine Rift Programme**
Maps, photographs, and information on protected areas and endangered species can be found here.

▶**Bushmeat Project**
On this site, read about one of the major threats facing gorillas today: the sale of bushmeat.

▶**Columbus Zoo**
Learn more about the Columbus Zoo's efforts to save mountain gorillas.

▶**A Conservation Triumph: The Mountain Gorillas of Rwanda**
At this site, find out how one person can change the world.

▶**Creature Feature: Mountain Gorillas**
Rwanda's mountain gorillas are seen through the lens of *National Geographic*.

▶**The Dian Fossey Gorilla Fund**
This organization is working to save the mountain gorillas of Africa.

▶**Fauna and Flora International**
This international conservation organization is a partner in saving gorillas.

▶**Forced Off Their Land**
This UN article surveys threats to mountain gorillas.

▶**Forest Conservation Portal**
On this site, learn about threats to the world's forests.

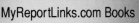
Report Links

The Internet sites described below can be accessed at http://www.myreportlinks.com

▶ **Frontline: Ghosts of Rwanda**
This PBS site examines the 1994 Rwandan genocide.

▶ **Global Species Programme: Mountain Gorilla**
Read about the endangered mountain gorilla at this WWF site.

▶ **Gorillas Continue to Get Caught in Snares**
From this report, find out about some of the methods that poachers use to trap gorillas.

▶ **Gorillas in the Midst of Extinction**
At this NASA site, learn about the role of satellite imagery in protecting gorilla habitat.

▶ **Great Apes and Other Primates: Gorillas**
Get the facts on gorillas at this Smithsonian Web site.

▶ **Great Apes Survival Project (GRASP)**
This site has extensive information on the survival of great ape populations worldwide.

▶ **International Fund for Animal Welfare**
The International Fund for Animal Welfare seeks to save endangered wildlife.

▶ **The Living Landscapes Program**
This program helps people learn how to share the earth with wildlife so that both benefit.

▶ **Mapping and Monitoring the Forests of Central Africa**
To learn more about the mapping of a protected habitat, visit this site.

▶ **Mountain Gorilla Protection: A Geomatics Approach**
Learn more about how mapping technology is helping preserve the gorillas' mountain habitat.

▶ **Mountain Gorillas**
This British site offers an overview of mountain gorillas.

▶ **Nursery in the Mountains**
Read the story of two gorillas living on a mountain.

▶ **Reports From the Field**
Learn about the work of the Mountain Gorilla Veterinary Project.

▶ **TRAFFIC**
On this Web site, read about the illegal international trade in animals.

▶ **USFWS Endangered Species Program Kids Corner**
This USFWS Web site offers ways you can help save endangered species.

active conservation—The term Dian Fossey used for her efforts to protect the gorillas within the park by keeping people out and stopping poaching.

anthropoids—Animals within the primate group that share certain characteristics, including the ability to move their fingers individually.

anthropologist—A scientist who studies human beings and their ancestors through time.

antipoaching patrols—Teams of people that find and destroy traps set by poachers.

belch vocalization—Purring, stomach-rumbling noises that gorillas seem to use to communicate that everything is fine.

cough grunt—A gorilla vocalization that sounds like a short, sharp bark from deep within the chest. Gorillas cough grunt to indicate displeasure.

DNA (deoxyribonucleic acid)—The basic material in the chromosomes of cells; DNA molecules carry genes transmitted from parents to their offspring, which result in inherited characteristics.

dominance—A rank of importance in an animal family. In a gorilla family, the dominant male is entitled to the best food, the best place to sleep, and the right of way on a path, among other things.

duiker—A small African antelope.

eastern gorillas—One of two gorilla species. The two subspecies of eastern gorillas are eastern lowland gorillas (also called Grauer's gorillas) and mountain gorillas.

ecotourism—Tourist programs designed to protect the ecology of natural environments.

foliage—Leaves, stems, and roots of plants.

genocide—The systematic killing of a group of people because of their race or ethnicity.

gorilla tourism—Programs that bring tourists to watch gorillas in their natural habitat.

habituate—To make gorillas comfortable enough with humans so that the gorillas can be studied and so that tourists can see them.

Hominidae—The scientific family classification of erect two-footed primates that includes humans, chimpanzees, gorillas, and orangutans.

Karisoke—A research station to study mountain gorillas established by Dian Fossey in Rwanda's Parc National des Volcans in 1967.

knuckle walking—The way gorillas walk, using feet and hands with fingers folded under.

Mountain Gorilla Project (now the International Gorilla Conservation Programme)—A plan to save mountain gorillas by putting an end to poaching, educating Rwandans about the value of the gorillas and the Virunga rain forest, and bringing tourists to Rwanda to see the gorillas.

primates—An order of mammals characterized by hands with opposable thumbs and fingernails instead of claws, binocular vision, and large brains. Humans, apes, monkeys, and related animals such as lemurs and tarsiers are all primates.

silverback—Term for an adult male gorilla that has a silver "saddle" across his back. The silvery hair is much shorter than the rest of his shaggy black hair. Younger males between nine and about fifteen years old are called black backs.

Chapter 1. Surprising Survival

1. Bill Weber and Amy Vedder, *In the Kingdom of Gorillas: Fragile Species in a Dangerous Land* (New York: Simon & Schuster, 2001), p. 51.

2. Dian Fossey, *Gorillas in the Mist* (New York: Houghton Mifflin, 1983), p. 83.

3. Ibid., p. 87.

4. Weber and Vedder, p. 365.

5. George B. Schaller, *The Year of the Gorilla* (Chicago: University of Chicago Press, 1968), p. 30.

6. "The Conservation Action Program: Eighteen Months After Inception," *The Dian Fossey Gorilla Fund International,* September 2002, <http://www.gorillafund.org/cont_frm/crnews/cap18moslater_sept02.html> (June 16, 2005).

7. "Gorilla Conservation," *Wildlife Conservation Society,* n.d., <congogorillaforest.com/congoconservationchoices/congogorillaconservation> (March 24, 2005).

8. "Cross River Gorillas," *World Wildlife Fund,* n.d., <http://www.worldwildlife.org/gorillas/subspecies/cross_river.cfm> (July 28, 2005).

9. Wildlife Conservation Society, "Gorilla Conservation."

10. Kelly J. Stewart, *Gorillas* (Stillwater, Minn.: Voyageur Press, 2003), p. 13.

11. Schaller, p. 8.

12. Ibid., p. 113.

Chapter 2. Being a Gorilla

1. George B. Schaller, *The Year of the Gorilla* (Chicago: University of Chicago Press, 1968), p. 5.

2. Ibid., pp. 34–35.

3. Ibid., p. 105.

4. Dian Fossey, *Gorillas in the Mist* (New York: Houghton Mifflin, 1983), p. 63.

5. Bill Weber and Amy Vedder, *In the Kingdom of Gorillas: Fragile Species in a Dangerous Land* (New York: Simon & Schuster, 2001), p. 118.

6. Kelly J. Stewart, *Gorillas* (Stillwater, Minn.: Voyageur Press, 2003), p. 23.

7. Schaller, p. 123.

8. Weber and Vedder, p. 51.

9. Stewart, p. 39.

10. Weber and Vedder, p. 52.

11. Ibid., p. 114.

12. Ibid., p. 50.

13. Schaller, pp. 35–36.

14. Fossey, p. 64.

15. Weber and Vedder, p. 121.

16. Fossey, p. 67.

17. Stewart, p. 28.

Chapter 3. Threats

1. Bill Weber and Amy Vedder, *In the Kingdom of Gorillas: Fragile Species in a Dangerous Land* (New York: Simon & Schuster, 2001), p. 127.

2. "Range States," *International Gorilla Conservation Programme,* n.d., <www.mountaingorillas.org/gorillas/ gorillas_range.htm> (June 8, 2005).

3. "The CIA World Factbook: Rwanda," p. 3, May 17, 2005 <http://www.odci.gov/cia/publications/factbook/geos/rw.html> (June 6, 2005).

4. Weber and Vedder, p. 107.

5. Ibid., p. 142.

6. Ibid., p. 334.

7. The CIA World Factbook, "Rwanda," p. 2.

8. Weber and Vedder, p. 348.

9. "Virunga National Park," *UNESCO World Heritage Centre,* May 25, 2005, <whc.unesco.org/pg.dfm?cid+31&id_site+63> (May 25, 2005).

10. Weber and Vedder, p. 348.

11. Stefan Lovgren, " 'Gorillas in the Mist' Park Slashed by Squatters," *National Geographic* News, July 12, 2004, <http:// news.nationalgeographic.com/news/2004/07/0712_040712 _mountaingorilla.html> (June 7, 2005).

Chapter 4. "No One Loved Gorillas More"

1. George B. Schaller, *The Year of the Gorilla* (Chicago: University of Chicago Press, 1968), p. xii.

2. Dian Fossey, *Gorillas in the Mist* (New York: Houghton Mifflin, 1983), p. 1.

3. Farley Mowat, *Woman in the Mists: The Story of Dian Fossey and the Mountain Gorillas of Africa* (New York: Warner Books, 1987), pp. 22–23.

4. Fossey, p. 12.

5. Ibid., p. 53.

6. Ibid., p. 125.

7. Mowat, p. 58.

8. Fossey, pp. 27–28.

9. Mowat, p. 60.

10. Sy Montgomery, *Walking With the Great Apes* (Boston: Houghton Mifflin Company, 1991), pp. 138–139.

11. Fossey, p. 173.

12. Ibid., p. 177.

13. Ibid., p. 26.

14. Mowat, p. 119.

15. Ibid., p. 293.

16. Ibid., pp. 286–287.

Chapter 5. New Directions for Gorilla Conservation

1. Bill Weber and Amy Vedder, *In the Kingdom of Gorillas: Fragile Species in a Dangerous Land* (New York: Simon & Schuster, 2001), p. 140.

2. Ibid., p. 143.

3. "History of the Mountain Gorilla," *World Wildlife Fund,* n.d., <http://www.worldwildlife.org/gorillas/subspecies/mountainTimeline.cfm> (August 24, 2005).

4. Liz Williamson, Ph.D., Director, Karisoke Research Center, "Mountain Gorilla Tourism: The Costs and the Benefits," Dian Fossey Gorilla Fund International (DFGFI), <http://www.gorillafund.org/cont_frm/fieldnews/fldnews_20010702.html> (August 24, 2005).

5. Weber and Vedder, p. 169.

6. Ibid., p. 177.

7. Ibid., p. 193.

8. Ibid., pp. 216–217.

9. Williamson, DFGFI.

10. Weber and Vedder, p. 140.

11. Williamson, DFGFI.

12. *World Heritage Nomination–IUCN Summary: Bwindi Impenetrable National Park (Uganda),* (IUCN, 1994).

13. United Nations Environment Programme, Protected Areas Programme, "Draft Revision, Bwindi Impenetrable National Park, World Heritage Site," n.d., <http://www.unep-wcmc.org/sites/wh/bwindi.html> (August 26, 2005).

Chapter 6. Gorilla Survival in the Midst of Turmoil

1. Bill Weber and Amy Vedder, *In the Kingdom of Gorillas: Fragile Species in a Dangerous Land* (New York: Simon & Schuster, 2001), p. 314.

2. "The CIA World Factbook: Rwanda," p. 2, May 17, 2005, <http://www.odci.gov/cia/publications/factbook/geos/rw.html> (June 6, 2005).

3. Weber and Vedder, p. 344.

4. Annette Lanjouw, "Building Partnerships in the Face of Political and Armed Crisis," *International Gorilla Conservation Programme,* n.d., <http://www.mountaingorillas.org/pdf/conflict_paper.pdf> (October 3, 2005).

5. "History of the Mountain Gorilla," *World Wildlife Fund,* 2005, <http://www.worldwildlife.org/gorillas/subspecies/mountainTimeline.cfm> (May 31, 2005).

6. Weber and Vedder, p. 348.

7. "History of the Mountain Gorilla," *World Wildlife Fund,* 2005, <http://www.worldwildlife.org/gorillas/subspecies/mountainTimeline.cfm> (May 31, 2005).

8. Marilyn Berlin Snell, "Gorillas in the Crossfire," *Sierra,* November/December 2001, vol. 86, issue 33, p. 7.

9. "The Karisoke Research Center," *Dian Fossey Gorilla Fund International,* n.d., <http://www.gorillafund.org/006_conserv_frmset.html>(October 4, 2005).

10. "Tourism in the Realm of the Mountain Gorilla," *International Gorilla Conservation Programme,* n.d., <www.mountaingorillas.org/gorillas/gorillas_tourism.htm> (March 28, 2005).

Chapter 7. Hope for the Future

1. George B. Schaller, *The Year of the Gorilla* (Chicago: University of Chicago Press, 1968), p. xi.

2. "Census Finds Mountain Gorillas Increasing: Virunga Volcanoes Gorilla Population Grows by 17 Percent Since 1989," *Wildlife Conservation Society,* n.d., <http://www.wcs.org/353624/192030> (March 24, 2005).

3. "The Karisoke Research Center," *Dian Fossey Gorilla Fund International,* n.d., <http://www.gorillafund.org/006_conserv_frmset.html> (October 4, 2005).

4. Ibid.

5. Annette Lanjouw, "Transboundary Natural Resource Management: A Case Study in the Virunga-Bwindi Region," International Gorilla Conservation Programme, November 2002, <http://www. mountain gorillas.org> (October 4, 2005).

6. Dian Fossey Gorilla Fund International.

7. Lanjouw, "Transboundary Natural Resource Management: A Case Study in the Virunga-Bwindi Region."

8. "Mountain Gorilla Veterinary Project," *Morris Animal Foundation,* n.d., <http://www.morrisanimalfoundation.org/apply/studies/mgvp/current.asp?section=0,0> (August 24, 2005).

9. "Partners in Conservation," *Columbus Zoo and Aquarium,* n.d., <http://www.colszoo.org/Conservation/pic/pic1.htm> (August 24, 2005).

10. "Improving the Livelihoods of Communities Around the Parks," International Gorilla Conservation Programme, n.d., <http://www.mountaingorillas.org/our_work/our_improving.htm> (August 25, 2005).

11. Leon Marshall, "Under Fire, World's Park Rangers Seek Protection," *National Geographic News,* September 5, 2003, <http://news.nationalgeographic.com/news/2003/09/0905_03 0905_parkrangers.html> (August 26, 2005).

12. "Ubuzima, a 13-Month-Old Reintroduced to Her Group," December 2002, *Gorilla Journal* 25, Berggorilla & Regenwald Direkthilfe, December 2002, <http://www.berggorilla.de/english/gjournal/texte/25ubuzima.html> (March 21, 2005).

Bodnarchuk, Kari. *Rwanda: A Country Torn Apart.* Minneapolis: Lerner Publications, 2000.

Gilders, Michelle A. *The Nature of Great Apes: Our Next of Kin.* Vancouver, B.C.: Greystone Books, 2000.

Green, Carl R. *The Gorilla: A MyReportLinks.com Book.* Berkeley Heights, N.J.: MyReportLinks.com Books, 2004.

Lewin, Ted, and Betsy Lewin. *Gorilla Walk.* New York: Lothrop, Lee & Shepard Books, 1999.

Mara, Wil. *Dian Fossey: Among the Gorillas.* New York: Franklin Watts, 2004.

Matthews, Tom L. *Light Shining Through the Mist: A Photobiography of Dian Fossey.* Washington, D.C.: National Geographic Society, 1998.

Oghojafor, Kingsley. *Uganda.* Milwaukee: Gareth Stevens, 2004.

Sloan, Christopher. *The Human Story: Our Evolution From Prehistoric Ancestors to Today.* Washington, D.C.: National Geographic, 2004.

Stewart, Kelly. *Gorillas: Natural History and Conservation.* Stillwater, Minn.: Voyageur Press, 2003.

Taylor, Barbara. *Apes and Monkeys.* New York: Kingfisher, 2004.

Taylor, Marianne. *Mountain Gorilla.* Chicago: Heinemann Library, 2004.

Turner, Pamela S. *Gorilla Doctors: Protecting Endangered Great Apes.* Boston: Houghton Mifflin, 2005.

Verrengia, Joe. *Cenzoo: The Story of a Baby Gorilla.* Boulder, Colo.: Roberts Rinehart, 1997.

Willis, Terri. *Democratic Republic of the Congo.* New York: Children's Press, 2004.